Super-
baby
Cook-
book

by Donna Lawson and Jean Conlon

Beauty Is No Big Deal

by Donna Lawson

Brothers and Sisters All Over This Land

Mother Nature's Beauty Cupboard

When You Can't Go Naked . . .
Here's Clothes to Sew on Fast

Super-baby Cook-book

DONNA LAWSON
& JEAN CONLON

Macmillan Publishing Co., Inc.
NEW YORK
Collier Macmillan Publishers
LONDON

Library of Congress Cataloging in Publication Data

Lawson, Donna.
    Superbaby cookbook.
    Bibliography: p.
    1. Infants—Nutrition. I. Conlon, Jean, joint
author II. Title. [DNML: 1. Cookery. 2. Infant
food—Popular works. 3. Infant nutrition—Popular works.
WS120 L425s 1974]
RJ216.L36   649′.3   73–13169
ISBN 0–02–569500–2

Macmillan Publishing Co., Inc.
866 Third Avenue
New York, N.Y. 10022
Collier-Macmillan Canada Ltd.

First Printing 1974

Book designed by Constance T. Doyle

Printed in the United States of America

To the Superbabies

Peter Conlon and his friends
Koz (Magic Mama's boy)
Maria-Theresa-Casale and her kid sister Samantha
Bipidy
Savitri Brightfield
Aya Murata down the block
Alexandra Posen in her loft on Spring Street
Jack in our nation's capitol
and Big D, Dylan Gary, out in L.A.
Eben in the woods
Aimee Swift on the road
Jill and Jonathan Radding from Larchmont
Maya
Donna's goddaughter Kristin
and her two sisters' kids:
Little Rossie, Mikie, Carol Ann, Erik, and Lisa
Peter's Cousin Teddy
Amanda and Marisa
plus:
Amanda and Marisa's mommy
and all the other mommies
and dear Grandma Conlon . . .
and Sandy the dog, of course.

Contents

What Baby Eats

Appendix

Introduction

Every parent wants a superbaby; perhaps not in size, weight, or even ability—but in health. The greatest gift that a parent can provide is to make it possible for the child to become an independent person, an individual. To do that, good health is needed, and super-health is a bonus.

Each cell that forms, grows, and multiplies becomes part of the person, and each cell is nourished by the food the infant, toddler, or child eats. This book directs itself to the child-feeder—mother, father, grandparent, babysitter, foster-parent, or anyone who is responsible for baby nourishment, and anyone who cares. It begins where feeding should begin, at the breast, and it sensibly, logically, and clearly follows the developmental stages of child growth through those first important weeks and months of the baby's life.

The first year of a child's life is a time of transition for the parent, too. *Superbaby* takes that into consideration. What good is a book that cannot be *used,* is too complicated to implement, or too complex to follow? This is a book which I can recommend and will recommend to all my patients. It is clear, accurate, useful, reassuring, and calm. It brims with good sense and good advice.

A toast—of whole wheat bread—to *Superbaby*.

Dr. Marvin S. Eiger

Super-baby Cook-book

Preventive Nutrition or Why Make Your Own Baby Food?

What you feed your baby from the time of his conception through to the time he's eating table food will determine his physical and even emotional well being for the rest of his life. Strong stuff this statement. But more and more concerned nutritionists, obstetricians, and pediatricians have come to believe that a good prenatal diet and careful nutritious feeding of infants can prevent heart-breaking damage to the fetus and to the growing infant.

The specialists in childhood development go so far as to say that a correct diet can affect intelligence, social stability, and general health. Feeding a child the right foods from the beginning can prevent a propensity for certain adult diseases such as hypertension and heart disease. And, as the days go by, more and more nutritionists are finding the causes of other diseases in poor eating habits that trace back to the crib. For just as you train your child to habits of good character you instill an affinity for nutritious eating. Chances are that good preventive nutrition—nutritionally setting the stage for a sound body and mind—will give your child a longer life, one that's healthy and happy enough to want to be prolonged.

Giving your baby lots of food, or the "best foods on the market" in good old American consumer fashion will not insure that he's being well fed. This is a sad fact, of which we are only recently aware. Although we are the wealthiest nation, we are not the best fed, for wealth follows up on enterprise. And enterprise in America's food industry has unfortunately meant the development of "convenience food": over-processed, over-refined, foodless foods packed with additives to give bolder taste and more salable texture and appearance and to insure a shelf-life that lasts longer than any of us wants or needs.

The average American adult consumer of convenience foods will this year eat four pounds of additives, more than one thousand of which have never been tested by the food industry or the FDA (Food and Drug Administration) although many have been tested by concerned scientists who have pointed out the damage of many of these additives. The food industry contends that only a minute quantity is put into each processed food. But certain additives can cause birth defects, cancer, and other frightening interference with life and health when taken in large doses. And who's to say how much of each additive we repeatedly eat in one food or in several foods? How much of a harmful additive can a human body, especially a youngster's small one, tolerate?

Next time you shop take a look at the labels on your foods. Notice the strange chemical sounding names that appear and reappear. Trace the names to a few of the recent reports written on food additives. When you learn what you are eating over and over again, it may shock you into returning to foods that are as close to their source as possible. When you buy a bunch of carrots at the supermarket you fairly well know exactly where it came from. Not so, a can of carrots. Who knows what it's been through before arriving at your table.

Ralph Nader and his raiders, God bless them, have fought the food industry and the FDA and made us aware that we should fight too. We can no longer look at Big Mama food industry to feed us, or Big Daddy government to protect us. We must assume the responsibility ourselves for what we eat and feed our children. Big Mama and Big Daddy are too busy protecting their profit margins at great cost to our welfare and the welfare of our children.

Commercially prepared baby food is big business—over \$400 million a year, the second highest profit in American food industry; citrus products rates first position.

The baby food industry has been willing to go to all lengths to protect this gargantuan profit, even to jeopardizing the health of the very little people who eat its products. Twenty years ago prepared baby food may not have been all that bad, maybe not good, but not bad. After World War II when the costs of vegetables and meats began to rise, the baby food manufacturers began to decrease the nourishing contents of its products replacing them with nutritionless fillers: water (the major ingredient in almost all of these commercially prepared foods), starch, and sugar.

When it was found that a baby's saliva left in a partially eaten jar of baby food would continue to "digest" the starch in the baby food making it appear spoiled, much to the consternation of the mother (who might therefore be lost as a customer), the baby food industry "modified" the starch.

The modified starch is never completely broken down by the infant's saliva (this was the point), therefore it follows that the immature digestive systems of infants never fully digest this food. Funny thing for a baby food industry to do, wouldn't you say?

As for sugar, it's entirely without food value—99 percent sucrose, pure calories, with no vitamins, minerals, or other nutrients. It contributes to tooth decay and to obese babies with an eating habit pattern set to continue obesity throughout their adult lives. It establishes an inclination to diabetes, hypoglycemia (a low blood sugar condition, caused by high sugar intake), and arteriosclerosis in later life. We have become a nation of sugar consumers (the per capita annual consumption in 1971 was one hundred pounds) whereas a couple of centuries ago, sugar was as rare to the average man's diet as truffles.

The baby food industry protected its income by adding these valueless, harmful fillers to its products. But it was to go even farther, looking away from the damage it was doing to youngsters, looking to the dollar.

The fillers did not taste very good; that is, they did not taste very good to mother who bought and tasted the food she fed her baby. But who's to say if baby could tell the difference between one taste and another? Certainly, not baby. Mother, the taster, was the all-important consumer to bring the baby food industry to today's $400 million mark. Therefore, mother's taste buds, not baby's, were appealed to with flavor enhancers. Salt, in proportions questionable for adult tolerance, were added: five to six times as much salt in baby meats as in fresh table meats, and six to sixty times as much in prepared baby vegetables as in fresh. This high salt content is maintained in commercial baby foods although recent research has shown that a large intake of salt in infancy may result in the development of high blood pressure in the adult.

Then there is monosodium glutamate, the additive which may have precipitated the downfall of the baby food industry. This additive was found to cause brain lesions and eye damage when tested in baby mice. Yet the baby food industry had been "testing" out this additive on human babies since World War II. And no one told mothers of its harm until Ralph Nader revealed it. Due to his hounding, MSG is no longer used in baby food production, although a few bottles manufactured before October 1969 may still be sitting on your grocery shelf waiting for your baby.

The elimination of MSG from commercial baby foods is a start. But what about sugar, salt, and modified starch? And even if they were eliminated, what would be left? Water? Well, not more than that. Just look what you're getting. Witness the label. Take that gourmet treat Creamed Potatoes and Ham (with bacon): water, diced ham loaf (boneless ham, water, salt, sugar, and smoked flavoring), ham flavoring (a mixture of artificial flavoring and garlic powder), smoked ham, dehydrated potatoes, bacon, soya protein, whole milk solids, citric acid, celery extractives, sodium nitrate, and modified starch. Yum.

Distinctively missing from the label is how much meat, the major food ingredient, is in the products. At least manufacturers of dog food inform the consumer by listing the quantity of meat on each can's label. The baby food industry doesn't even pay you that courtesy because it would be admitting there's very little meat in it.

The tragedies of feeding your infant commercially prepared baby food don't stop with the additives, flavor enhancers, and lack of decent food content. Unfortunately no.

Doctors in West Germany and Canada have found, for example, a startling correlation between an intake of nitrate in certain commercially prepared baby foods and a disease called methemoglobinemia, which reduces the oxygen in the blood causing labored breathing and in severe cases suffocation, particularly in the first three months of life. Apparently, nitrate (a chemical fertilizer used to replace nitrogen in depleted soils) is converted to poisonous nitrate in infant canned foods such as spinach, peas, beets, and green beans when the cans or jars are opened and exposed to certain bacteria in the air for a day or two before using. This bacterial conversion may also occur when the aforementioned vegetables are frozen and left unthawed for a couple of days before cooking. The nitrate content in *fresh* spinach, peas, beets, and greens is not harmful as they contain an insignificant amount of poisonous nitrate. Evidently the toxic nitrate level (when it converts to poisonous nitrate) develops somewhere between harvesting and use, probably on opening the jar and letting it sit.

Then there is the problem of jars of baby food whose caps have thoughtlessly been removed by shopping mothers checking by smell "the freshness" of the baby food. When replaced, the cap's previous removal is not discernible to the next mother who comes along, nor is the possible presence of bacteria, maybe fatal salmonella, caused by the food's exposure to air.

We realize this is hardhitting, not a soft, mellow introduction to baby food. But a milder approach might not convince you, the mother of a beautiful infant, of *your* responsibility in preserving your baby's health and well being.

We are, after all, fighting many years of commercial baby food advertising which extolled the convenience of its products. Jean is a busy career woman, as well as baby Peter's mother. And both of us, who are avid supporters of the rights of women, would never advocate a mother sacrificing herself to the kitchen whether to prepare baby's or the entire family's meal. But, how inconvenient can it possibly be to go to the refrigerator, pick out fresh vegetables, fish or meat, a carton of yogurt, and some fruit? They're all the same foods shopped for for the rest of the family (if you've planned it right). And how inconvenient can it be to cook the food for the entire family, baby, too, with adherence to the best nutrition you know? To that very end, this book, in the following chapters, intends to bolster your knowledge of nutrition and suggest other good nutrition books as well.

Nutritional cooking, we might add, doesn't take additional time to do, but it can make all the difference to your family's health. Nutritional cooking, for example, means decreasing, even sometimes eliminating, saturated fats from the family's diet. Saturated fats—butter, some margarines, chocolate, animal fats, all of which harden at room temperature —have been found to raise the blood cholesterol level and contribute to heart disease. Nutritional cooking is waterless cooking where vegetables and fruits are cooked in a minimum of time in as little water as possible to retain important vitamins and minerals which might otherwise be destroyed by overcooking, heat, and water. Nutritional cooking is cutting down or out on the salt, grease, sugar, and refined grains, and processed convenience foods. And, it means reading labels beforehand to determine the food content and the bad properties, such as additives, which you may be getting in your food.

Baby's food is an addendum to good nutritional planning for the entire family. Baby's meal comes from the main table. Once the family meal is prepared you remove a portion of the food for baby, put it in the blender and let it whrrrrr. How much trouble is that?

Isn't it more inconvenient to lug jars and jars of "convenient" baby food home from the supermarket? Isn't it quicker to turn on the blender than to read the depressing labels on the jars of commercially prepared baby food? And isn't it less expensive to make your own baby foods than to buy over-priced commercially prepared baby foods? Consider the price of a jar of prepared strained banana, 13¢. Whereas a single fresh banana costs approximately 5¢ or 6¢. And what is there to straining a banana? You peel it, mash it with a fork, maybe add a healthy additive like yogurt.

But, even if you don't think it's more convenient or less expensive to make your own baby food, can you afford not to set your youngster on the right track in life with a good preventive nutritional foundation, one that will help him through his early years and in later life be the healthiest, most stable adult you could possibly launch on life?

Shocking, but true in America's age of afflu-ence: as our gross national product increases our proper dietary habits decrease and have steadily been decreasing for more than ten years. The higher the income, it seems, the poorer the diet. Middle class families with their cupboards and refrigerators filled with all the latest "convenience" foods are more un-dernourished than societies in our country and elsewhere who eat whole grains, fresh vegetables, and fruits grown in enriched soils, maybe in the family's own garden plot, and whose mothers breast feed their infants because to do otherwise would be too expensive. But there's a growing majority of our children suffering the affects of nutritional deficiencies. They don't get adequate placental nutrition before they are born. Their diets are lacking after they are born and may not improve (unless mothers change the tide) as they grow into adult life.

Infant nutrition is serious business. Start now to make your own healthy, wholesome, nutritious baby food. Don't you want a superbaby?

PS: The authors of this book are as concerned about the rights of females as those of infants, female ones most definitely included, and apologize for the consistent use of the masculine pronoun he. By tradition, and you see how deeply we are entrenched in it, he is the editorial preference. You may take a pen and substitute she for he whenever he appears, if yours is a daughter and that is your choice.

Baby Is What Baby Eats

A rundown of baby feeding from time of
conception through breast feeding to bottle
feeding to solids . . . on to all the nutritional
facts you need to know about baby food . . .
plus equipment . . . plus storage, planned
menus, and ways to make all this easy
for mom.

When Does Baby Start to Eat?

The fact is: All babies start to "eat" well before they're even born. They rely on nourishment from the moment of conception to grow, to build, to develop, to be. The food his mother eats is as important to a fetus as milk is to an infant, as solids are to his older sister or brother. So when you ask when does a baby start to eat, you've got to go way way back to before baby is born.

WHAT YOU EAT

You may already know that the nourishment of your child begins while he's still a growing fetus. But did you know you begin to nourish your prospective infant even before he's conceived? The fetus will take his body-building nourishment during the crucial early weeks spent in your womb. The mother's body provides the fetus with the appropriate vitamins and minerals to help it develop through the various stages of growth. These stages begin when the sperm first introduces itself to the ovum and produces a fertilized egg. Therefore it's never too early to consult your doctor on the subject of nutrition as soon as you think you *might* be pregnant. Then continue to take his advice throughout your pregnancy.

AND CONTINUE TO EAT

Pregnancy is no time to diet. Eating the right kinds of foods is very important when you're pregnant because every day of your pregnancy your baby is growing inside you. Each day different parts of the baby's body are forming. Some countries recognize this growth by regarding a baby as being one year old on the day of his birth.

BUT WHAT TO EAT?

Every pregnancy is different. For this reason only your doctor is qualified to give you an appropriate diet. He will recommend how much weight you should gain and what foods to eat. Your doctor will also instruct you on your general health goals during pregnancy.

MOTHER'S WEIGHT, BABY'S HEALTH

During the sixties a ten- to fifteen-pound weight gain during pregnancy was considered sufficient for both cosmetic and health reasons. Recent scientific research has found that a ten- to fifteen-pound gain is insufficient and may actually contribute to fetal malnutrition. At the recent symposium on nutrition and fetal development sponsored by the March of Dimes, a twenty-five pound or over gain was recommended. Today this weight is considered adequate to produce a big, healthy, full-term baby. Less of a weight gain could produce a premature infant. And a malnourished fetus may also be limited in physical and mental development.

During pregnancy don't fill up on such forbidden goodies as pizza, soda, cornbread, beer, wine, salted nuts, and whipped cream. When you stuff yourself with these foods which have little or no vitamins or minerals, you will have no room left for foods a pregnant woman really needs: meat, fish, vegetables, cheese, milk—all the body-building proteins. One quart of milk per day, about one half pound of lean meat, even more, plus four servings daily of bread or cereal and ample vegetables add up to a well-balanced prenatal diet.

WHEN TO EAT

Many women feel bloated after meals, particularly in the early months of pregnancy. Consequently, they begin to cut down on their food intake, again a threat to the health of the fetus. It's simple enough to save yourself the misery of "the bloats" and still nourish your unborn child. Cut down on the amount eaten at each meal and increase the number of times you eat each day. Six meals a day, even more, are easier to digest than three. Just be sure each meal is well balanced, contains proteins, minerals, and vitamins.

FOODS TO AVOID WHILE PREGNANT

During pregnancy if you wish to avoid excess water retention, known medically as toxemia, limit your intake of salt and sodium. Salt ranks high in bacon, ham, salt pork, salt fish, chipped beef, and other salty prepared meats, dark rye bread, potato chips, popcorn, pretzels, olives, meat sauces, and the like. Sodium content is very high in such foods as pickles, mustard, ketchup, ice cream, pizza. Monosodium glutamate is so high in Chinese foods many doctors won't even let their pregnant patients walk the streets of Chinatown. They fear they'll pick up too much MSG, known as the Chinese Restaurant Syndrome.

NO FROM THE NO LIST

Alcohol and cigarettes can be harmful to your own health at best, but can retard the growth of the fetus as well. Better to kick the habit of pre-dinner cocktails and after-dinner smokes than expose your unborn infant to unnecessary risks. As for smokes, marijuana can be extremely harmful to your unborn child. Psychedelic drugs can produce chromosome damage. And you only need to look at the evening news to see the sad effects of narcotics on infants whose mothers introduced the habits to their unborn fetus. At birth these babies are hooked.

Don't take anything that has not been prescribed by your doctor especially for you during this pregnancy. Look on any pill, powder, tablet, capsule, liquid medicine, or home remedy as a possible danger to your baby—unless the doctor prescribes it. Check with him early about the safety of any prescription you had before you became pregnant. Never touch medicines prescribed for other members of your family or for friends.

Avoid everything on this list unless your doctor orders one or more to treat a condition you have discussed with him: patent medicines, pep pills, laxatives, tranquilizers, aspirin or any other pain reliever, mineral oil, diuretics or water pills, baking soda, antacids, nerve tonic, sleeping pills.

BUT WHAT ABOUT VITAMIN AND MINERAL SUPPLEMENTS?

Some doctors are avidly against taking vitamin and mineral supplements during pregnancy. Others feel that most diets are inadequate without them. Vitamin D, for example, has been known to cause abnormalities in infants. An excess of vitamin D supplements can be toxic. No more than 400 units per day should ever be taken in supplemental form. Standing or walking in the sun, if there is available sun, can provide a beneficial amount of natural vitamin D. When Jean was pregnant, she sunbathed in her bikini up until Peter was born; terrific vitamin D for both mother and baby by osmosis according to her obstetrician.

Vitamin A supplements must be kept to 25,000 units per day. Vitamins C, B$_6$, and K have also been investigated as causes of fetal abnormalities. In natural food form, brewer's yeast and wheat germ are terrific sources of the B vitamins, while bone meal is an excellent source of calcium and molasses a source of iron.

Many obstetricians believe that 5 mg. of folic acid should be taken daily. This B vitamin is the most common nutritional deficiency during pregnancy. But as yet folic acid can't be obtained without prescription although scientific investigation indicates lack of this vitamin in a pregnant woman can hinder the development of her fetus.

FOOD FOR THOUGHT

What you feed your mind when you're pregnant is as important as what you feed your face. Don't listen to old wives' tales, ad infinitum, from Aunt Myrtle about her in-a-family-way days. Aunt Myrtle's intentions may be harmless but her drama-filled stories about the medieval tortures of a World War I delivery room can be inaccurate in retrospect and downright scary. There's plenty of good, helpful information around about pregnancy and birth. Your very own doctor may recommend some reading matter on the subject. Hospitals have prenatal classes you and your husband can attend. Or write to the March of Dimes. They'll be more than happy to send you their free publications on pre-natal care. Write:

The National Foundation—March of Dimes
Box 2000
White Plains, New York 10602

Breast Fed Is Best Fed

The breast fed baby is the best fed baby. Unfortunately the majority of American mothers are either unaware of this fact or choose to ignore its implications. A shockingly low percentage of babies in the United States are breast fed. Only one out of four infants *ever have any* breast milk. Of that 25 percent, the greater majority of these infants are not breast fed after their first five days of life. In other words, by the time most babies leave the hospital they are totally bottle fed.

How sad that so many, many babies are being

denied their most basic right of life—breast milk. Can supposedly loving mothers ignore all the nutritional and psychological benefits breast feeding offers their dependent babies? Can they in good conscience give their infants formulas which at best can only imitate breast milk? What can their rationale be? We can only conclude that these mothers are simply uninformed. All mothers should at least know what they are denying their child *before* they make the decision to do so. A mother-to-be should make it her number one responsibility to learn the facts about breast feeding.

WHY BREAST MILK?

Breast milk is always at the right temperature. Cow's or goat's milk must be refrigerated at cold temperatures and warmed to room temperature before it can be served to infants.

Breast milk is more easily digestible than milk from other mammals, as it forms soft, easily assimilated curds in the infant's stomach, whereas large, heavy cow's milk curds are difficult for baby's digestive system to handle. Goat's milk curds are smaller and more easily digestible than cow's milk. But mother's milk is still the most digestible of all.

THE COMPOSITION OF BREAST MILK

Mother's milk has all the nutrients an infant needs for the first few months of life—enough proteins, fat, lactose, vitamins, and minerals except for two. Neither cow's (unless fortified), goat's, or mother's milk have enough vitamin D for the infant. Baby must get this vitamin from the sun or through vitamin drops. And no milk has enough iron. So at about age four or six months the infant's diet must be supplemented with this necessary mineral.

Many of the nourishing benefits a youngster gets from breast milk comes from what mother eats. Large amounts of the mother's calcium intake, for example, go toward building the baby's bones.

Your doctor will prescribe a specific diet while you are breast feeding. It will be rich in proteins, vitamins, and minerals. The diet will consist of meat, poultry, fish, or eggs for protein, leafy green and yellow vegetables and fruits for minerals and vitamin C, cereals or bread for B vitamins, and fortified milk or supplements for vitamin D. The amount of sugar, starches, and fats needed will depend on your individual weight.

Speaking of the content of breast milk, there's always the question of DDT infiltrating mother's milk. Formula feeding advocates correctly point out that breast milk has a high content of DDT.

True, but cow's milk does as well, although not as much as breast milk. This is the fact of the matter: Sad as it may be, our environment is now full of DDT. DDT is in everything from the air we breathe to the soil in which we grow our foods. So why eliminate the good benefits of breast feeding your baby? Why deprive the infant of the nourishing and psychological assets of mother's milk?

BREAST MILK DEVELOPS NATURAL IMMUNITY TO DISEASE

Regular breast milk is blue in color and thin in composition and begins to secrete on the third day after birth. Before that deep yellow colostrum is released. Colostrum is thicker and different in chemical composition than later milk. It contains more proteins, minerals, vitamin A, and nitrogen, less fat and sugar than the regular breast milk. Colostrum is easy for baby to digest as he is adjusting to the world those first few days. It also has a slight helpful laxative effect on him. But best of all, colostrum contains antibodies which make the infant immune to certain diseases. Studies prove that breast fed infants have fewer colds, are subject to fewer digestive upsets, have less colic and fewer cases of diarrhea than bottle fed babies.

BREAST FEEDING AND ALLERGY PREVENTION

Breast fed babies are less susceptible to allergic problems once they go off the breast (see Testing for Allergic Reactions, p. 38). Occasionally some food the mother is eating may bring on allergic reactions such as diarrhea, hives, skin rash, or vomiting. But once this food is traced through the mother's diet the allergic reaction will stop.

BREAST FEEDING AS AN EARLY PREVENTION OF HEART DISEASE

Recent investigations indicate that breast feeding may be a deterrent to arteriosclerosis in later life. Breast fed babies, in fact, have higher blood levels of cholesterol than bottle fed infants, but these levels drop toward the end of the first year of life when the infant is weaned to solid foods without the step of bottle in between.

Doctors encourage breast feeding even with the indication of high cholesterol in mother's milk. Their studies show that an elevated cholesterol level during the first critical months of life seems to touch off some regulatory mechanism that might help keep a person's cholesterol level down later in life.

BREAST FEED TO PREVENT FATTIES

Breast feed your infant and he's less likely to turn out a fat kid. Overweight adults have too many or too large fat cells as do obese chidren. These children tend to have been heavy since their first year of life. This overweight tendency usually was caused by overfeeding at this vunerable time. Too many fat cells that first year will make it difficult ever to lose weight. Breast feeding regulates food intake and avoids your force feeding baby, a tendency brought on by bottle feeding or too early an introduction to solids.

BREAST FEEDING AND EMOTIONAL STABILITY

Educators feel the emotional security developed in the breast fed infant is reflected in a child's later educational development. Breast fed children are more attentive in school, have a quicker rate of reading comprehension than bottle fed children and appear more agile and coordinated in physical activities. It has been suggested that the switching back and forth of the baby from one breast to another helps develop good eye coordination and general physical balance, thereby explaining the child's noticeable achievements during his school years.

IN ADDITION

Information on breast feeding can be obtain by writing for literature from: La Leche League International, Franklin Park, Illinois 60131. Or read, *The Complete Book of Breastfeeding* by Marvin S. Eiger, M.D., and Sally Wendkos Olds (New York: Workman Publishing Co., 1972).

Bottle Feeding

Suppose you don't breast feed. There are reasons why women don't. Mothers who have been ill during pregnancy can't physically afford the added burden of breast feeding. Other mothers have jobs outside the home which are so demanding that no time is left for breast feeding. Active career women often breast feed their infants in the early months before returning to their offices and work out a combination of breast and bottle thereafter. Some women just frankly don't like the idea of breast feeding for one of a number of reasons. This being the case, they should not be pressured into it. Their nervousness and uptightness about breast feeding will convey itself to the child and this may be worse than not breast feeding. Aside from that, why make yourself miserable? No kid wants an anxious mother. He'd sooner have a bottle.

If you decide not to breast feed, you'll be giving your baby a formula in a bottle. Even when you breast feed it's a good idea to give a relief bottle to your baby by the time he's a month old. This serves two purposes. First, it gets the baby used to the bottle should it be necessary to wean him to it before he's ready for a cup. Second, it gives you an opportunity to be away from your baby occasionally and this will be good for you.

BOTTLE FEEDING EQUIPMENT

Contrary to what the baby supply advertisers will feed you, the paraphernalia needed for bottle feeding is quite minimal. You will need:

1. six four-ounce glass or plastic bottles with wide mouths (note: Fill up to the neck of the bottle so baby doesn't swallow air);

2. one dozen nipples, six or so with single punctured hole openings for infant feedings so that the liquid flow is regulated, the remaining nipples with "X" perforation opening for junior drinks;

3. six bottle caps to cover nipples

   during outings;
4. one bottle brush for cleaning bottles;
5. a pan for warming formula;
6. some air-tight jars for storing extra drinks.

Many of these items you will most likely have among your everyday kitchen equipment and won't have to purchase especially for baby.

MILK FACTS

You may think milk is milk. But just take a look at the choice of milk in the supermarket. It's overwhelming. There's whole fluid fresh milk. There's concentrated, there's condensed, there's evaporated milk. What's pasteurized? What's homogenized? What's raw milk? What does it all mean?

In a nut shell: Today most milk goes through the processes of pasteurization and homogenization. (The only milk that doesn't go through these processes is raw milk. This is certified to meet government standards.) Pasteurization is a heating then cooling process which destroys harmful bacteria. Homogenization breaks up fat particles in whole milk and disperses them throughout.

There are several types of milk. *Whole fresh fluid milk* contains no less than 3.25 percent milk fat and no less than 8.25 percent milk solids not fat. It's pasteurized and homogenized or raw. Health food advocates feel that raw milk is best because pasteurization destroys a certain amount of nutrients in milk. Raw milk is bottled right from the cow. There're some mothers and doctors who claim they won't feed a kid raw milk without knowing the cow personally.

Skim milk is fresh fluid whole milk with the fat removed to reduce cholesterol and calorie content. As skim milk greatly reduces calorie intake and may undernourish the infant, it's not wise to give it to baby until he's eating solid foods to balance this lack. Even then check with your doctor.

Fortified milks have been enriched by increasing their nutrient content with vitamins A or D, multivitamin preparations, minerals, lactose, and nonfat dry milk. Fortified milk is made with whole or skim milk.

Soft curd milk is modified so the curd tension is less, thus softer than average cow's milk globules. This apparently makes the milk easier for infants to digest.

Concentrated fresh milk is whole milk which has had two thirds of the water removed under vacuum.

Evaporated milk is fresh whole milk concentrated by removing half its water under vacuum. It is sealed in a can and heat sterilized to prevent bacterial spoilage. A can of evaporated milk requires no refrigeration until opened.

Dry whole milk is made of fresh fluid whole

milk from which water has been removed. The concentrated milk is sprayed into a drying chamber. As it comes in contact with heated filtered air, most of the remaining water evaporates and the solids fall to the bottom of the dryer. When reconstituted, the dry milk has the same nutrition value as regular whole milk.

Nonfat dry milk is made of fresh fluid whole milk from which both water and fat have been removed by the same process as the dry whole milk. When reconstituted it has the consistency of skim milk.

Sweetened condensed milk is fresh whole milk that has had part of the water removed under vacuum. Sugar is added, accounting for 40–45 percent of this product's total weight. The sugar concentration inhibits bacterial growth so cans need not be heat treated nor refrigerated until opened. *The high sugar content in sweetened condensed milk prohibits its use in infant formulas. Don't confuse it, as many people do, with evaporated milk which is also sold in cans and is used in infant formulas.*

TYPES OF FORMULAS

The pediatrician will decide the specific formula and milk needs of your baby. But generally you can expect formulas to be some variance of milk plus milk sugar (lactose) plus boiled water. Formulas are made with whole milk in either liquid, powdered, or evaporated form. For children with digestive problems, skim milk, goat's milk, or yogurt-based formulas are used. For babies allergic to dairy products, meat-based formulas, bone meal, and soy formulas are given. And a vegetarian baby has a formula all his own: It's a mixture of tahini, a highly digestible sesame seed butter, diluted with boiled water.

Premixed commercial formulas attempting to simulate breast milk are also available. They are ready to use or need diluting. If powdered, they are mixed with water. Be leary of premixed formulas where the source of the water isn't specified on the label. Some water is high in nitrates, dangerous to tiny infants in large doses (see Water, p. 58).

BEWARE OF IMITATION MILK

Certain fluid milk-like products packaged in the same type of container as fresh fluid milk are marketed in many grocery stores. The American Academy of Pediatrics is concerned that these products, with fat bases of partially hydrogenated coconut oil, may be mistaken for fresh whole or skim milk and used in baby's formula. The academy warns such milk may stunt infant growth. These imitation milks are inferior substitutes for those other milks which are the major dietary source for growing infants.

From Liquids to Solids

Babies and mothers who enjoy breast feeding can continue even after junior is in walking shoes, if they both like. However, somewhere between four and six months, the baby's iron supply built up prenatally by the mother begins to play out. As milk—breast, cow's, or goat's—is insufficient in iron the child needs supplemental food to give his rapidly growing body sufficient strength.

Baby will usually let you know when he needs solids. He may suddenly increase his feeding demands. When he continually wants to be fed, in spite of more frequent feedings it's a good indication it's time for solids. It's also possible, if the infant is closer to four months, that he isn't overly hungry, but merely feels a cold coming on. Or, he may be tense for some reason and just wants to cuddle up to his mom.

IRON, FIRST AND FOREMOST

The first source of iron an infant eats is likely an egg yolk mixed with cereal. Bear in mind, however, that eggs are one of the commonest causes of infant allergies. Should an egg affect him adversely, put off giving it to him until he's one year old. Substitute liver, puréed in the blender with broth. Iron rich brewer's yeast can be used to fortify his formula.

WHAT TO FEED BABY WHEN

Feeding schedules vary from infant to infant. You and your pediatrician will decide on a final food routine. We have consulted several pediatricians and nutritionists and have established the following sequential order for the recipes in this book, all tried by our head tester, Peter Conlon:

fortified drinks	about 3 weeks
yogurt	about 6 weeks
fruits	about 6 weeks
eggs	about 4 months
cereals	about 4 months

vegetables	about 4 months
meat and fowl	about 4 months
fish	about 7 months

HOW MUCH TO FEED BABY WHEN

Specific quantities of foods to feed baby are not unlike feeding schedules—each varies from infant to infant. Your neighbor's baby may be eating two bananas a day at the same time yours can only handle a half, at most. But then, maybe your baby started on four ounces of orange juice a day when his buddy was only having a dropper full. In both cases, each baby is obviously getting his daily requirement of vitamin C, although each from a different fruit, one in a solid, one in a liquid form.

This is not to make how-much-to-feed-baby-when a mind boggling project. But, just to give you an idea of approximately how much a baby can be expected to consume (by the time he's been introduced to all the basic baby food solids, around seven months, or so), we've included the following "quantity list" of foods. A child should have each one daily in order to obtain the necessary nutrients his always-growing body requires:

> milk—3 eight-ounce bottles
> juice or fortified drinks—2 eight-ounce bottles
> yogurt—3 ounces

fruits—2 ounces each of two or
   more fruits
eggs—1 whole or 2 yolks every other
   day or so
cereals—2 to 3 ounces once or twice
   a day
vegetables—2 ounces each of two
   or more vegetables
meat or fowl—2 ounces
fish—2 ounces

TEACHING BABY TO EAT

Just as you taught baby to suck the breast or bottle,
you'll now teach him to eat solids. This isn't easy
as he'll try to suck the spoon. This will be frustrating
to him. He's hungry and doesn't want to fool around
learning something new.

To combat his confusion for the first few weeks
offer solids between nursings or directly after feedings. Then baby will be somewhere in between full
and hungry.

In the beginning use a small spoon with just a
tiny amount of food on the tip. Hold baby in your
lap tilting him back slightly then touch the spoon
to his lips and drop the food in. Remember, you are
introducing him to solid food not filling him up.

At first it will seem as if you are either nursing,
bottle feeding, or solid feeding all day long. This

always-feeding schedule may drive you a little crazy. But, relax, soon enough things will get easier as baby weans over to a mostly solid diet. Before long he'll eat more food per meal and need less feedings per day.

Before you know it, baby will move on to "finger foods"—solids he'll want to feed himself. Cut up table foods into small size portions, place on the high chair tray, sit back, and let junior have a go at it. These days require a lot of patience from mommy. Junior will mush the food around, try it out with a smell or two, lick it, push it into his mouth, spit it out, and start all over again.

TESTING FOR ALLERGIC REACTIONS

Each new food is introduced allowing four or five days in between them. This way any allergy that shows up can be traced to the appropriate food, and eliminated from the infant's diet. Give each new food a week before introducing another. Start with ¼ teaspoon and increase the amount a bit every day until he gets all he wants. He'll let you know when he's had enough. He just won't eat any more. Any food already introduced should be given to the child again in another four or five days. He may show an allergic reaction to it this time, even if he didn't the last. The first year, it's smart to repeat foods every few days to try and spot an allergic reaction.

INFANT APPETITE

Appetite varies with children. It can change daily. One day baby may love sweet potatoes and then be totally put off by them. But don't give up on these or any other foods he turns his nose up at. Most likely he'll be gobbling them up again next week. Still you may turn up with a food finicky kid and it's a good idea to be prepared ahead. Introduce as many different foods as possible, so you'll have some left to choose from when he begins voicing opinions and spitting out the foods he doesn't like. Even when left with only five or six foods on his preference list, provided they aren't lopsided nutritionally, you're still okay.

DEMAND FEEDING

Eating schedules per se should all be thrown out the window. Feed infants on their demand (so comes the expression demand feeding), even if it means every two hours around the clock. As baby gets older, off breast and onto bottle and solids, don't set up a breakfast, lunch, and dinner menu. Such regimented feedings are socially acquired eating habits of adults and have nothing to do with baby feedings. Baby should be served three, four, or more meals a day. In no way should you force food on a child, and set him up to be a fattie for life.

Once baby has been introduced to solids, you'll soon be able to offer him almost anything the rest of the family eats as long as it isn't heavily spiced, sweetened, too rich, or heavy on the vino.

WHEN BABY WON'T EAT
A SOLID THING

Before you pat yourself on the back over your success with baby's first solids, be aware of this: There will be days when baby won't eat anything solid. Don't frustrate yourself or your baby if he decides not to have his solids. His failure to eat may not constitute an off day. He may feel fine, but have something more important to do at meal time—like building ABC blocks—and he doesn't want to get down to something as boring as mommy's idea of a gourmet meal. He might give you a minute or two in the high chair, but chances are he'd rather keep right on playing.

When you see that kind of impatience coming on—head for the blender, push the whip button. Throw in the puréed food, add a liquid that will be palatable (2 parts liquid to 1 part purée), and let it whrrr. Put baby's dinner in a bottle and serve. You'd be surprised how a not too successful scrambled egg breakfast can turn into a delicious midmorning brunch.

Baby's Off Days

Sometimes when a youngster gets sick, you have to work with what you have on hand until you can reach the doctor. What you have on hand may not be medicinal (we would not be so presumptuous as to suggest any medicines), but baby foods which have worked wonders for children. After all, food was used as a cure-all before anything else. And maybe that's the reason why so many people today are going back to natural foods and herbs to find health and an overall feeling of well being. Hippocrates, the father of medicine, said centuries ago, "Your food shall be your medicine." He may have had something there.

If you think back on your ethnic origins you might come up with some food remedies of your own. Did your English mum serve you mint or fennel tea, or your Puerto Rican mother soothe your aching tummy with some Old Hen Chicken Soup (chicken broth), or when you couldn't get anything else down remember that delicious hot bowl of pastina from your mama mia?

Some of these food remedies aren't just about mommy being nice. They actually do soothe aching stomachs basically because all these foods are easy to digest.

Indigestion is more often than not the reason for babies' discomfort. One of the earliest solids, if not the first, for some babies are fruits. If served raw, fresh ripe fruits can cause diarrhea. The introduction of any new foods often results in either constipation or diarrhea. It's a good idea to introduce new foods early in the day rather than at dinner. Then you'll have the afternoon to sooth an uncomfortable, squalling youngster, not the night.

DIARRHEA AND CONSTIPATION

Diarrhea in a baby is when there is competely unformed stools. This means the bowel movement is liquid. Note that even on good days, babies have very loose stools.

Nutritionists recommend steamed carrots for calming diarrhea. Bananas often work, too. But don't play around with diarrhea if it doesn't straighten out in a day. Get the doctor. When diarrhea appears in a small infant there can be serious, even dangerous loss of fluid in a short time.

Constipation is the opposite extreme of diarrhea. The stool is hard, dry, and painful to pass. A baby is not necessarily constipated when he doesn't move his bowels for days. This is not unusual for either breast or bottle fed infants. Yet many mothers panic when their babies don't have a bowel movement for one day. They confuse infant's with adult's regularity.

Jean remembers a time when Peter had not moved his bowels for five days. She was sure her baby would explode. Her doctor reassured her that many babies go without moving their bowels for days on end. However, he felt five days was long enough. His recommendation of a four-ounce bottle of prune juice did the trick. Peter was back to "schedule" pooing away daily as he had done before.

Yogurt is a natural food remedy for both constipation and diarrhea. It is the most digestible of all baby foods, can be given to baby as a solid or liquified and mixed with his formula. It breaks down foods into digestible forms, helping the body manufacture large quantities of vitamins B and K, thereby making it almost impossible for disease-producing bacteria to live within the digestive tract. In other words, yogurt a day keeps the doctor away.

VOMITING

There're two kinds of vomiting. One's a burp. Don't take that too seriously, because babies often give a nice healthy burp after a gluttonous meal. Consider the small spit-up as a compliment to your cooking. However, a more serious form of vomiting which should be brought to the doctor's attention is called projectile vomiting. This vomiting occurs when baby throws up and out his meal. That you must be concerned about. Call the doctor. It could be the beginning of a flu, it might be an allergic reaction to the food you're feeding the baby, or any one of a number of other physical causes. We're not going to try to analyze it. Nor should you. *All projectile vomiting requires doctor's attention.*

Food Allergies

Food allergies vary from uncomfortable incidences to chronic situations. Finding the bad-guy food and eliminating it from baby's diet is usually the solution to the following problems.

ECZEMA: ACIDIC JUICE REACTION

When it comes to eczema, highly acid fruit juices sometimes cause irritation to sensitive skin. It may help to cut down on baby's intake of orange juice and tomato juice during the rash break out.

PROTEIN RASH

When little ones have had a high protein intake they sometimes bloom in a horrid blotchy rash around the diaper area, in back of knees and elbows, or as blotches on little puffy cheeks. This can happen when a baby has had an egg plus meat plus whole milk all in one day. Cut down on the proteins.

COLIC

There's a theory that colic is a protein allergy, as it occurs at a time when the digestive tract is introduced to foreign proteins like cow's milk. Some foreign proteins even reach breast fed babies through their mother's milk. This theory is based on the fact that colic often stops when the mother or infant's diet is changed or his formula modified. Sometimes it works to switch from a formula of fresh pasteurized milk to evaporated milk, or even a meat base, soy, or sesame formula. Some milk allergic infants are breast fed until they can tolerate cow's milk.

CELIAC DISEASE

This chronic condition is caused when the child's intestines are unable to handle fats or gluten, the protein in wheat, rye, and barley. This intolerance is characterized by frequent diarrhea which lasts for several months and can gravely weaken a young child. It appears at the end of baby's first year and continues into his second. To treat it a doctor usually recommends throwing out the culprit foods and setting the baby on a diet of skimmed milk, cottage cheese, and ripe bananas. Little by little other food may be added as the infant's appetite improves, his bowel movements become more solid, and his pediatrician approves.

MULTIPLE ALLERGIES

Some infants are raised entirely without milk, even mother's milk. Jean's niece, Maria Theresa Casale, has never had the real stuff in her life. Both her parents have long medical histories of allergies. When Anne, Maria's mother, was a teenager she was receiving thirteen shots a week for every kind of allergy. There was a shot for the next door neighbor's horse allergy, one for the soft down pillows on granny's bed, and a whole lot for food allergies. So Maria's pediatrician, for precaution's sake and Maria's, never even tried Maria on real milk, or her mother's milk for that matter. He didn't want to take a chance of allergic reactions. Charles, her daddy, is asthmatic. That medical fact just made for one more possibility that Maria would be born with a built-in hereditary allergy to food, animals, dust, etc. So Maria was raised on a milk-free diet. Now age eight, Maria has become a perfect example of a healthy well-fed child brought up milkless. It's possible, and following are some of the substitutes which made it so.

> soy milk formula instead of milk formulas
> juice instead of milk
> carob instead of chocolate
> egg yolks instead of egg whites
> yellow vegetables instead of green vegetables

And then Anne eliminated wheat flours, breads, and cereals totally from Maria's diet.

THE PEDIATRIC ALLERGIST

More and more childhood ailments are found to be
rooted in allergic causes. So much so many pediatricians have become "pediatric allergists." If your
child suffers from eczema, asthma, or gastric dis-
turbances, make this specialist your best friend.
Children usually don't outgrow allergies. For this
reason it's essential to find their origins and eliminate
them from your baby's life for his physical and
psychological comfort. Work with your allergist to
establish a custom made-to-order diet for your allergic child.

SUGGESTED READING LIST

The following books are comprehensive and helpful
to mother in understanding the source and possible
solutions to minor and chronic infant problems:

> *Dr. Benjamin Spock's Baby and
> Child Care,* Hawthorn Books
> *Your Allergic Child* by Herman
> Hirschfeld, M.D., Arc Books, Inc.
> *The Allery Cookbook* by Carol
> G. Emerling and Eugene O.
> Jonckers, Doubleday & Company,
> Inc.

Teeth, Teething, and Tiny, Sensitive, Sore, Red Gums

If there ever was a tooth fairy it was old ma who ate the right food while little Superbaby was floating in embryonic bliss. During the late months of his incubation, he already had teeth. Granted they were underneath his gums, but they were teeth nevertheless. Mother's diet during baby's incubation had a lot to do with the later growth and development of those baby teeth. Insufficient protein in mama's diet caused the infant's teeth to be smaller, erupt later, and decay more. If her diet was short on calcium and vitamin D her child would tend to teeth cavities; short on vitamin A the youngster's teeth enamel would not form correctly.

WHEN AND WHERE DO TEETH APPEAR?

A tooth does not have to be visible to be a tooth. It starts to play havoc with baby before it erupts. Some fortunate babies come through teething without the slightest discomfort. But for most kids and their parents, who must suffer their whining and whimpering along with them, teething is sheer hell.

Most books will tell you baby will begin his cranky days of teething at around four months or so. But some babies begin teething as young as six weeks to two months. And some kids' teeth appear two by two like animals on Noah's ark. So you can imagine the discomfort they feel.

The first two teeth come in at center bottom. Then four erupt at center top. Baby usually has these six teeth by his first birthday. That's why his diet should be high in calcium, protein, vitamins C and D, and especially magnesium right from the start.

PACIFIERS

During teething, bib after bib will be filled with drool and everything from mommy's rollers to daddy's tools will be in baby's mouth. This is the time to whip out a good old pork bone to chomp on. Even if baby isn't on junior foods, he'll love to chew bones just like a puppy.

To sooth really sore, red gums give baby nice cold foods such as yogurt or, if the child is on junior food and still has teeth coming in, give him any one of the ices (see p. 162). The cold acts as a mild type of novocaine substitute somewhat numbing gums to pain.

If you want, give your youngster an aspirin to soothe his pain. Follow directions from your doctor and use the given quantity mixed in with fruit purées. Or dab a cotton ball in daddy's bourbon, whisky, or scotch and rub it on baby's gums to give temporary relief.

Don't buy baby a teething ring as he can puncture it with a finger or a tooth that has grown in and swallow the enclosed liquid.

Avoid teething crackers, biscuits, or cookies since tooth care today pays off in cavity-free teeth tomorrow. Not only do they add up to fat food eating, but an unnecessary oversupply of sugar detrimental to teeth enamel.

A rubber pacifier helps sooth teething pain. But sucking a bottle as a pacifier could cause tooth decay by bathing the upper front teeth in milk or juice. This is the opinion of the New York Dental Association.

For God's sake, every day a child is cranky or downright irritable don't shove it off on an old wives' tale that goes somewhat like this: "Oh, he's only teething!" A whining baby is not necessarily a teething baby. A kid can teethe for four months to two and a half years. So be attentive. Something else could be bothering him.

PREVENTIVE DENTISTRY

Breast fed infants often get fluorides through their mothers, but then they go on to juices and formulas and fail to continue with it. Yet fluoridation reduces chances of dental decay up to two-thirds. The American Dental Association says you can't start your child early enough on fluoridation, as tooth enamel is formed during the first eight to twelve years of life. You can buy fluoridated pills on doctor's request if it's not in local water.

CLEANING BABY TEETH

Up to the time of baby's first dental visit remove bacteria-laden plaque deposits from gums and erupting teeth by regularly cleaning them with gauze. Continue this practice until baby is old enough to brush his own teeth.

Certain foods act as natural cleaners and are best for children a year or older who can handle junior food and have tiny teeth to clean. These are meat bones, celery, and carrots: sugar free and high in protein, minerals, and vitamins. When walking or running with these hard foods in his hand, he could trip, fall, and perhaps choke on them. This is not to scare you, but merely a gentle precaution. Give such foods to baby while he's in his high chair.

THE CHILD'S BITE

Dentists and pedodontists are presently studying the

effect of long-time bottle feeding on the development of a child's bite. Apparently, by thrusting his tongue against the front teeth each time he swallows, a learned procedure to keep the milk from drowning him when he's lying on his back or side, baby can malform his bite. The only way to avoid this thrust is to hold a child upright while on the bottle, as though he were breast feeding.

THE DENTIST'S CHAIR, BEYOND SORE, RED GUMS

At three years, Superbaby goes for his first dental visit. At this point X rays can show all his permanent teeth. Introduce the dentist as a friend. Make a dental visit a threat and the child will be likely to consider it that the rest of his life.

The ABC's of Baby Food Nutrition

What you feed baby now will not only affect him for the next year or two but for the rest of his life. For now he needs body-building energy foods to help him maneuver his way around the crib, then sit up, crawl, stand, walk, run, talk, and expand his world. Later he'll carry over into adult life the good eating patterns you've established for him as an infant.

At first baby gets the nutrients he needs from breast milk, cow's or goat's milk. Although milk will always remain important in his feeding, at about four months the youngster needs the addition of vitamin C and iron for the most part found in solid foods.

When on a diet of solid foods baby will need nutrients from each of the following categories daily.

> proteins
> fats
> vitamins
> carbohydrates
> water
> minerals

PROTEIN: THE BODY-BUILDING FOOD

Protein is found in meat, fish, eggs, milk and milk products, and to a degree in vegetables, grains, and nuts. It's necessary to the healthy growth of the embryo and later to the development of the infant in the outside world.

Proteins are essential to growth and repair of

body tissue: muscular, bone, skin, blood, and nerve. Each tissue is made up of cells which are made up of protoplasm which is, in fact, protein. Food protein restores body protein. The protein that baby eats builds and repairs the different protein-composed cells of his body.

Protein is needed to sustain the energy level of the child. The faster he moves the quicker he reduces his protein level. As the growing baby is moving plenty fast he needs a lot of protein. For most of the first year of his life he gets the protein he needs in milk. After that he gets part of his protein from sources other than milk.

HIGH PROTEIN FOOD FOR BABY

These are the lean meats (this includes the glandular meats: liver, heart, kidneys, sweetbreads, and brains), fish, fowl (turkey and chicken), eggs, cheese (including pot, farmer, and cottage cheese), milk, and yogurt.

LOW PROTEIN FOODS FOR BABY

These are grains, beans, peas, nuts. In order to get the daily requirement of protein, low protein foods (that is, foods lacking in one or more essential amino acids) must be supplemented by high protein foods, which are complete. Your baby could not get enough protein in a daily diet of beans and nuts, for example. But if his diet were supplemented with milk and milk products, he'd be just fine. Then, he'd be called a fancy name like a lactovegetarian.

CARBOHYDRATES

These are the sugar and starches needed for energy. The infant begins his carbohydrate intake with milk sugar (lactose), then works up to health-giving sugars and starches in fruits, vegetables, molasses and honey.

Sweet fruits and vegetables make excellent sweeteners for baby's food. So do molasses and honey. Molasses is rich in iron; the darker variety has about fifteen times more iron than the lighter and about as much iron as you'd find in nine eggs. It contains as much calcium as there is in a glass of milk, and is 50 percent natural sugar. A little molasses in an infant's formula gives him a lot of iron. Honey is a pure energy food, containing about 70 to 80 percent simple sugar, minerals, and vitamin B complex.

The nourishing starches are whole grain flours (particularly stone ground) and products made with these flours and vegetables such as potatoes, beans, and peas. Check labels on cereals, breads, pastas to see if they are made with whole grain flour. A frustrating check of your supermarket, although whole grain wheat products can be bought there, may send you to a health food store, or to your own oven. Many women are taking to baking and finding it extremely satisfying, not only nutritionally, but creatively.

Babies need the right carbohydrates to convert into body sugar which is stored in small amounts in the liver to be used for energy when the body needs it. The excess from worthless refined starches and sugars is stored in fat deposits anywhere the baby's body can make room for it. Refined starches and sugars aren't a source of energy; they only produce a fat, unhealthy kid.

FATS AND OILS

A certain intake of fat is necessary for energy, good skin, hair, and nails. There are two kinds of fat: unsaturated and saturated. At first the infant takes his fat from milk. This is saturated fat as is all fat from mammals. Unsaturated fats are oils from fish, safflower, soybeans, corn—all oils which after heating stay liquid at room temperature. After the baby is off mother's milk or formula, unsaturated fats are preferable to saturated fats such as animal fat, butter, chocolate, some margarines—all fats which harden at room temperature after being heated.

WATER

Infants may drink as much as ten times the water per body weight as an adult. So how can you neglect knowing what's in that water? Water is an excellent source of minerals. So much so, that distilled water, bereft of any minerals, could cause a mineral deficiency in children. Unfortunately, misinformed mothers who think they are prescribing health for their children sometimes give them distilled water.

Mineral content in public drinking water varies from place to place. New York City's drinking water, for example, is supposed to be excellent (it also contains fluoride, good for teeth). Arizona's water has such a good high mineral content you could almost chew it. And in some places in southern California you need a faucet filter to siphon out the rocks— minerals no less. Some nutritionists suggest adding foods high in minerals (almonds, raisins, molasses) to water, then filtering out the solid materials after they have soaked in the liquid for a few days.

There are places in this country where the water is so permeated with virus the only way to make it pure is to boil it. This is, in fact, a necessary precaution to take with water given any infant up to two months old.

Chlorine is put into water to kill bacteria. Some people object to chlorine in water and give their families bottled spring water, which unlike distilled water has plenty of minerals. Unfortunately, bottled water has fewer regulations and standards than tap water. This is not to say it's unhealthy. It would just be better to have your doctor recommend a brand, or have it analyzed as you would your tap water.

In a few places the nitrate content of water, from chemical fertilizers which have sluffed off into wells, streams, and lakes, is so high it is dangerous for your infant. Nitrate poisoning is thought to be a contributing cause of infant cyanosis, a disease where the baby's body doesn't get enough oxygen. Now that's pretty scary.

The press usually lets the public know quickly when local water is in poor condition. But you can find out ahead of everybody else by having a sample analyzed at your local land-grant college, or at the state laboratory. This service only costs a nominal fee.

All this may seem to be pushing you to the borderline edge of hysteria. But investigating your water supply is a simple procedure. It's about time, you know, that we take things in our own hands. After all, we can't take our environment or our children's health for granted. We have to do something about it.

VITAMINS

Each vitamin does its own specific chore; this has been demonstrated by scientific research. Although the daily requirements have not been stated for most vitamins save for vitamins A and D, we know the child can get the necessary amount from a balanced diet of milk products, eggs, meat, fish, green and yellow vegetables (one of each daily), fruits, and whole grain cereals. There are limited requirements set on the amount of vitamins A or D in supplementary pill or liquid form, but you can't overdose on food.

There are fat soluble and water soluble vitamins. The former dissolves in fat, the latter in water. This is why vitamins C and B complex which are water soluble, not fat soluble, are not stored in the body and must be replenished every day. This is why vitamin C in vegetables is dissolved when they're soaked too long in water.

Actually, for nutritional value, raw vegetables would be preferable for baby if he could digest them. Raw juices, if you're lucky to own a juice extractor, are superb for baby's diet.

Vitamin A

Since this vitamin aids growth, it's very important to baby. It also gives him smooth clear skin, glossy hair, strong teeth, and eyes that see well in the dark. And, it helps to fight bacteria. This is a fat soluble vitamin most plentiful in fish oils; also fish, liver, eggs, cornmeal, whole milk, cheese, sweet potatos, carrots, apricots, apples, cantaloupe, and dark green leafy vegetables.

Vitamin B Complex

Nutritionists believe that the overprocessing of foods, especially the milling out of the wheat germ, has resulted in most youngsters being deficient in vitamin B. This is why it's important to provide the baby with whole grain cereals.

Wheat germ flakes, brewer's yeast powder, and yogurt, all strong in vitamin B complex, are easily added to other foods to fortify them with these essential vitamins.

The B complex contains thiamin, or vitamin B_1; riboflavin, or vitamin B_2; niacin; B_{12}; and the B_6 vitamin, pyridoxine. Other members of the B complex are pantothenic acid, folic acid, para-aminobenzoic acid, choline, biotin, and inositol. They are water soluble vitamins. Each does its task, but all must be in the diet, as one can't do its work without the other.

Thiamin, or B_1, strengthens the nervous system, helps carbohydrates convert into energy, and aids appetite. Brewer's yeast is a particularly strong source of B_1, which is also found in meat, peas, leafy green vegetables, and nuts.

Riboflavin helps baby to use oxygen most effectively, strengthens the functioning of his eyes, and promotes good skin. Again, brewer's yeast is a good source as are milk, liver, eggs, fish, poultry, and whole grains.

Niacin helps tissues in the proper use of oxygen and promotes body growth. The nervous system and mental health are also affected by niacin. Without this vitamin, riboflavin doesn't have the proper affect on the infant's body. Niacin is found in whole grains, green vegetables, lean meats, and poultry.

Vitamin B$_{12}$ helps the child's red blood cells form and aids the balance of his nervous system. Brewer's yeast, wheat germ, liver, eggs, milk, meat, and other animal proteins are great sources of this vitamin.

Pyridoxine, or *B$_6$*, aids development of the child's nervous system, builds strong red blood cells, promotes appetite, healthy hair and skin. B$_6$ produces adrenal hormones and antibiotics. These vitamins are in uncooked green vegetables and in spinach, cooked or uncooked.

Vitamin C

This is a water soluble vitamin. You probably know more about this vitamin than any of the others. For one, it helps stop colds and other infections, builds up baby teeth and gums and the connective tissues that help keep bones in place. This is the first supplement your baby gets after milk, either in orange juice or in a prescribed drop form. Oranges and other citrus fruits are particularly high in vitamin C. Vitamin C is also in tomatoes, cantaloupe, and leafy green vegetables. A less familiar source of this vitamin is rose hips. Rose hips is actually extracted from the fruits of the rose that grow after the petals have blown away. This liquid, available at drug or health food stores, mixes in with fruit purées, soups, or custards.

Vitamin D

Vitamin D helps prevent tooth decay and builds strong bones. Sunshine is the best source. If short on sunshine, feed baby fish liver oil. Ask your doctor the amount to give him. Vitamin D is also in liver, eggs, and raw and some fortified pasteurized milks.

Vitamin E

Vitamin E, you might like to know, is the sex vitamin, building fertility and reproductive aptitude. Never too early to cultivate it. Wheat germ, in oil or grain form, and other whole grains are loaded with it.

Vitamin K

Vitamin K is necessary for blood coagulations. It's found in liver, fresh vegetables, and yogurt.

MINERALS

The body of both the baby and the adult contains minerals: iron, phosphorus, calcium, sodium, magnesium, iodine, sulphur, and trace minerals. These minerals build strong bones, teeth, and gums; increase energy; create a calm nervous system; and regulate the thyroid. One mineral, phosphorus, is even said to increase intelligence.

These minerals need replenishing constantly. They are restored through baby's drinks (with almost all the minerals, but iron) and the food baby eats. The minerals reach the food through the soil. The soil determines the amount of minerals in the plants you feed the infant. The minerals in the plants the cow eats determine which will end up in her milk and the products made from her milk. The minerals in the food you eat determine those that will be in your milk when you nurse your infant. Anyway, it's God's plan. And if man will stop messing around with the ecological balance of our soil, our babies will get the mineral content they need to grow into strong healthy adults.

Calcium calms infant tantrums and helps form a serene disposition. Milk is the best source. In milk, calcium is combined with phosphorus, which must be present for calcium to be absorbed in the body. Supplemental bone meal is also a good source.

Phosphorus revs up brain cells and quickens impulses. It acts as a hardening agent for teeth and bones. It is in milk, yogurt, cottage cheese, eggs, poultry, lean meat, and fish.

Iron prevents anemia. Each body cell depends on it for oxygen. Egg yolk is high in iron, as is molasses, fish, brewer's yeast, wheat germ, almonds with skins on, grapes, raisins, and apricots.

Iodine helps regulate the thyroid which controls metabolism. Fish is high in it.

Sulphur purifies the bloodstream, builds strong nails, and makes hair shiny. The best sources are wheat germ, eggs, cheese.

Potassium has been used by doctors in cases of acute infant diarrhea to replenish the body's lost supply. Potatoes, fish, eggs, whole grains, meat, apples, and leafy green vegetables are good food sources.

Chlorine helps distribute hormones and aids muscle contractions. It is widely used in water purification. Best sources are leafy green vegetables and beets.

Copper aids iron in distributing oxygen throughout the body. It also helps formation of skin pigment. Copper is found in liver, sea food, egg yolk, apricots, whole grains, and leafy green vegetables.

Magnesium is important in the growth and maintenance of healthy bones and teeth and is found in whole grains, nuts, and leafy green vegetables.

Sodium cloride, or salt, is important to many of the body's metabolic processes. Salt is in meat, raw vegetables, eggs, and fruits. A few light shakes of table salt, preferably iodized, should be added to food. But excess salt can lead to high blood pressure as an adult.

Natural Additives

Usually baby's food will be blended to a purée or chopped to a coarser consistency (if he's junior age) right from the table food prepared for the family. Even when prepared especially for baby, the food's own natural juices may be enough to give the meal the smooth consistency infants prefer. But sometimes a natural thickener like arrowroot or thinner like fruit juice or smoother like yogurt will be desirable to improve upon the consistency of a puréed or ground food which is too grainy, or excessively runny. You and your baby will be the judges. Also, a natural thickener or thinner may be a healthy additive to enhance the nutritional value of a meal. The sweeteners, molasses for one, not only provide flavor for babies old enough to recognize the subtle taste difference, but also boost the iron content of the meal. Then there are the super supplements—bone meal, brewer's yeast, powdered milk, and wheat germ—which not only hearten baby's health, but the entire family's.

THICKENERS

Arrowroot starch is a highly digestive thickener, ground from the arrowroot; supplies calcium, potassium, and a reasonable amount of sodium; has an amazingly smooth consistency when mixed with water.

Cornstarch is removed from all the fibrous matter of corn by consistently washing and sifting it over fine silk sieves. It's easily digestible and a smooth thickener.

Whole grain cereals are perfect thickeners for over-blended, too watery baby foods (see Cereals, Porridges, and Plain Ol' Gruel, p. 122).

THINNERS

Fruit juice, fresh, is a good thinner (see Baby Drinks: Fruit Juices, Fruit Blends, Milk Pluses, and Milk Shakes, p. 93).

Fruit liquid from stewed fruits is full of retained vitamins which have seeped into cooking water (see Hello Fruits, p. 103).

Meat broths are rich in proteins, can be used to moisten dry meats or to blend into smooth purées (see The Meat Game, p. 139).

Milk, plain or fortified, is always a good thinner.

Milk formulas and milk pluses (see Baby Drinks:

Fruit Juices, Fruit Blends, Milk Pluses, and Milk Shakes, p. 93).

Vegetable juice can be obtained from a juicer if you have one. Lettuce juice, high in vitamins A, B, D and with large quantities of C, iron, potassium, calcium is recommended as an addition to bottled milk, as it gives the necessary vitamins and bone-building salt destroyed in pasteurizing milk. Mix with food or give to baby in a bottle, after feedings.

Vegetable liquid retains minerals leached out of vegetables by cooking them (see Vegies, p. 128).

SMOOTHERS

These foods mixed or blended with other foods are guaranteed to give a smoother texture to baby's meal:

Bananas are high in vitamins A, B, and C plus iron (see Hello Fruits, p. 103).

Cottage cheese is a good meat protein substitute, smooths out to a creamy consistency when blended with other baby foods.

Eggs are high in protein, iron, and vitamin A (see Eggs and Eggs In Things, p. 113).

Meat broths are rich in proteins, can be used to blend dry meats into smooth purées (see The Meat Game, p. 139).

Yogurt is rich in protein and helps produce the B vitamins (see Yogurt, Yoghurt, Yoghourt, p. 99).

NATURAL SWEETENERS

The purpose of using the following additives is not merely to sweeten but also to increase nutritional value of baby foods:

Honey, a source of natural sugar, some minerals, and B vitamins, is a pure energy food.

Molasses is very high in iron and has some minerals and B vitamins.

Sweet fruits with the exception of heavily fibrous or seeded varieties are good natural sweeteners (see Hello Fruits, p. 103).

Sweet vegetables, yams, squashes, carrots, and beets, for example, are valuable in carbohydrates, vitamins, and minerals (see Vegies, p. 128).

SUPER SUPPLEMENTS

The following foods are extraordinary in their nutritional value. For this reason they are desirable food additives for infants and toddlers, growing children, and other members of the family:

Bone meal is a floury, powdery substance ground

from cattle bones, is high in calcium, phosphorus, and trace minerals. It's a good supplement to mix with milk and other baby drinks.

Brewer's yeast is a by-product obtained in the beer-brewing process. It contains vitamin B complex, protein, minerals, carbohydrates, and fats. As a food supplement to mix with food and drinks, it's available at health food stores in tablet, powder form, and soluble flakes.

Miso is a soybean paste available in health food stores, rich in protein and hearty in flavor, which makes a nice addition to soups, vegetables, and fish dishes.

Powdered milk is a concentrated source of all milk nutrients and is an excellent supplement to add to infant foods.

Tahini is a sesame butter made from pealed sesame seeds which have been finely ground to a thin paste. It has been eaten for thousands of years and is a favorite food among vegetarians. Purist vegetarians or "vegans," that is, vegetarians who eat or drink no animal products at all, use it as a milk substitute. At times, tahini is also fed to milk allergic babies. High in protein and extremely digestible, tahini is delicious mixed with vegetables, or as a spread like peanut butter on whole wheat bread. Buy it at health food stores.

Wheat germ is the embryo of the wheat and the most nutritional part of it. Unfortunately this is the portion of the wheat that is milled out to produce refined flours and cereals. Wheat germ, rich in vitamins E, B complex, A, and fatty acids, is the highest known source of growth food benefits.

Baby Food Equipment and How to Use It

Practically everything you'll need to make food for your baby can be found in your own kitchen. The following is a suggested list. You can make do with less equipment. The most important item, perhaps the only one you need to buy, is a blender. On the other hand you could get by with a fork to mash the food and a wire whisk to beat it to a baby-soft purée.

BABY FOOD GRINDER

This may be used instead of or as well as a blender. One of the most popular brands is The Happy Baby Food Grinder designed by a doctor and available through Bowland-Jacobs Manufacturing Co., 9 Oakdale Road, Spring Valley, Illinois 61362. It costs approximately $5 and grinds one cup of food at a time. It grinds cooked meats and purées apples and other fruits without your having to peel them. Core, peel, and seeds end up in a little detachable compartment you can empty later. Consistency of foods, as with a blender, is changed by adding water.

BLENDER

There are many good brands of blenders, so shop around before making your decision. Prices range from $20 to $50. A blender will chop or purée most foods, but some have difficulty in grinding raw muscle meats and none will extract juice from fruits or vegetables. For that you'll need a fruit and vegetable extractor. If you want to go for the additional expense, see below. Blenders are easy enough to use: Each is packaged with an explicit direction book, or simply read the blender buttons and push whichever is appropriate (chop, mix, grate, purée, blend, liquify) to make each baby meal.

DOUBLE BOILER

This is useful to cook cereals smoothly and slowly and to keep them from burning.

JUICER

The juice extractor is a costly (about $70) addition to your baby food equipment and it's optional. But the benefits to baby and the entire family are terrific, if you can justify the expenditure. As you know, heat and water (both used in the preparation and packaging of commercial baby foods) destroy a large amount of the vitamin and mineral content of vegetables and fruits while raw vegetables and fruits retain their valuable food content. Try fresh extracted carrot juice and give some to junior. You'll never turn back. Again, comparison shop before deciding on one particular brand.

PRESSURE COOKER

The most important factor in cooking for baby is to preserve as many vitamins and minerals as possible. Of course, the less water used and the quicker the food is cooked, the more nutrients it will retain. The pressure cooker, costing $10 to $15, cooks food instantly with little or no water.

SAUCEPAN

If you don't have either a pressure cooker or a steamer rack, a stainless steel or heavy iron saucepan can be used for waterless cooking. For vegetables, for example, fill the pan two-thirds full. Then cover pan tightly with its self lid. Reduce heat to very low, and cook vegetables until tender. Cooking time varies from vegetable to vegetable: fifteen minutes for cabbage to an hour or more for beets.

SKILLET

This is used to braise meats before they are puréed or ground in blender or grinder. The best skillet for baby food cooking is made of heavy iron.

STEAMER RACK

This costs from $4 to $7 and is handy for steaming anything. It is a collapsible, perforated stainless steel contraption which fans out and sits in almost any pan to hold vegetables, fruit, or fish while it steams. Most vegetables take four to five minutes to steam, saving precious vitamins and minerals from drifting away in the water. The water left in the pan contains nutrients which have drained into it and can be put into baby's bottle or used to purée infant foods.

THE EXTRAS

None of the following equipment listed is a "must" for making your own baby food. However, all are certainly helpful utensils to speed up the process:

> colander—use to drain foods
>
> grater—use to grate foods
>
> measuring cups and spoons—use to determine quantity of ingredients
>
> mesh strainer or sieve—use to strain foods
>
> slotted spoon—use to remove solid foods from cooking liquid
>
> spatula—use to scoop out any remaining foods in blender, bowls, or pans
>
> stainless steel knife—use to cut, slice, dice, or chop baby food
>
> vegetable brush—use to clean raw vegetables and fruit
>
> wire whisk—use to hand whip liquids

Food Storage

There are basically two processes for storing baby food: canning and freezing.

CANNING

To our minds, canning is complicated and time-consuming, plus it's tricky seeing that the food doesn't spoil in the canning process. If you already know how to do it, fine. But it's not a project recommended to start during your busy days as a new mother. Also, you can't beat fresh food from the table, better yet fresh from the garden if you have one. Just throw the food in the steamer for a bit, then into the blender, and in a minimum of time you're ready to feed baby.

But some mothers recommend canning your own baby food. The ones we talked to suggested buying a pressure canner or some less expensive, simple canner model, costing around $6. You'll also need some additives such as sugar to preserve certain foods and ascorbic acid crystals for others. Those, plus can and/or jars for storage ought to round out your list of necessary canning equipment. Commercial canners come with directions which we recommend you follow since each type of food, fruits and vegetables, for example, require different types of preparation.

FREEZING

Freezing is by far an easier storage method to use, less time-consuming and less additional equipment required.

Set aside the foods you're going to freeze. Never freeze food that has been in baby's serving dish; the bacteria in baby's saliva will cause the food to spoil.

Cooked foods such as puréed meats or vegetables can be divided into meal-size portions (approximately two to three ounces per serving), placed in tightly sealed plastic refrigerator jars or wrapped in plastic wrap or waxed paper enclosed in airtight aluminum foil, and stored in freezer up to two to three months. Liquid foods such as soups and broths can be poured into ice cube trays, stored in the freezer until solidified, then removed and tightly sealed in plastic refrigerator bags. Place the cubes back in freezer and pull them out as needed. For quantity information—three to four cubes make approximately ⅓ cup of liquid. For foods that baby will eat within the next two days, put leftovers in plastic or Pyrex dishes, cover and store in the lower part of the refrigerator. It's always wise to date whatever food you store with the original preparation date.

NECESSARY EQUIPMENT FOR
BABY FOOD STORAGE

aluminum foil, plastic wrap, waxed
   paper
ice cube trays
labels (optional)
plastic and Pyrex dishes with tops
plastic refrigerator bags
pressure or ordinary canner
   (optional)
storage jars and cans

Mother Savers: Working Baby Food Preparation into Your Day

No more of this "I'm only human, I can only do one thing at a time!" Because now you're super-human, being a new mother and all, and must do several things at a time or you'll never get it all done in a day. Yet mothers are people, you know, and it's only a matter of a little organization to make that twenty-four-hour day work.

A DAY'S ONLY TWENTY-FOUR HOURS LONG

Baby care and baby food preparation have to be worked into your already existing hours since there is no possible way of adding more hours to your day. As much as all brand-new mothers would like to have a thirty-two-hour day, the fact is, there are only twenty-four hours, eight of which must be set aside for healthy sleep to cope with your active day, besides a half an hour here and a half an hour there for rest and nap time-outs needed espe-cially by the breast feeding mother. Then there are a few minutes or so that every woman justifiably wants to spend by herself reading, sunning, knitting, whatever. There's also the time you want to spend with your husband and the other children in your family, enjoying their company and letting them know that the new baby isn't mommy's everything. And, if you're a working woman, business hours cut down your available hours even further for doing all the things that need to be done from child care to making your own baby food. What time you're left with, if you're lucky to have any, is maybe an hour on the outside to spend in the kitchen among the ripe bananas, cauldron of homemade broths, and crocks of yogurt.

BE PREPARED FROM DAY #1

From the beginning (that means in your ninth month of pregnancy or while you're spending the week in the hospital after having junior), figure out how to work baby care into your already busy day. Get very specific; plan what to do with each hour of your day. Some of the following ideas you might find helpful for cutting corners or minutes off overly long household projects. Since infant's needs are so demanding, included are tricks to help you get from sunrise to sunset without disintegrating into an overworked and underthanked domestic laborer.

DOING A LOT IN A LITTLE TIME

There's no law saying you can't have a pot of stew stewing, a load of diapers going through a wash cycle, some chicken broth solidifying in an ice cube tray deep in the fridge, and be sponging the baby all at once. Everything but baby, you'll find, can more or less take care of itself.

When a baby's awake he pretty much takes up your undivided attention. When he's asleep for those two-hour spans, that's the time to fit in a million household chores. Cleverly call ahead to the butcher and place your order which you can pick up later when walking the baby, the dog, the parakeet, and yourself, giving everyone some fresh air. During baby's nap is also the best time to make baby food in quantities. Homemade applesauce takes a bit of doing (see p. 108), but certainly can be made at the same time you're concocting the chicken broth (see p. 144). Both are good baby foods to make up in batches and store for later use.

Generally speaking, you'll find you're more efficient during the times when baby naps than when he's awake and needs cleaning, feeding, hugging, and loving. Remember, you are his nurse, babysitter, playmate, companion, and mother all wrapped up into one. In other words, you're baby's supermom!

SETTING UP SHOP

As for making baby food, do set aside one shelf in the kitchen cabinet for baby bottles, a couple of silver cups, and some basic baby food equipment (see p. 71). It's easier to just grab for what you need than to have to stop and figure out what you did with the nipples or tongs. (It's also easy when the babysitter comes to have everything organized so that instructions can merely be: "All the stuff for the baby is on that shelf.") Of course, put things in logical places; bibs may be classified as clothing, but better store them next to bottles and blender in the kitchen than with the T-shirts and diapers in the baby's room. Basically such organization saves you time in the long run. Once you have those things needed for baby's care all in an easy to reach spot, then you've set up shop.

SHOPPING AND COOKING FOR BABY AND FAMILY ALIKE

Shop with foods in mind that both family and baby can eat. You'll notice in the following recipe section that recipes are often given for meals that can be adapted for both baby and adults. So shop for the needed ingredients with the entire family menu at hand.

There's no reason to cook separate meals for baby, except maybe mushing up a banana now and then. Like shopping, cook baby's meals right along with the rest of the family and in the process of becoming knowledgeable about making your own baby food, you'll simultaneously nutritionally improve meals for the entire family.

As was pointed out above, certain baby foods can be made in quantity, such as broths, which can be frozen in ice cube trays, then stored in airtight plastic bags for use at a future date. Yogurt, when you make your own, can be made in large quantities as it stores well and long, remains fresh for days on end. Applesauce can be made in advance and can later be blended and served with many other foods. However, you wouldn't have a lot of cooked squash on hand because a kid doesn't eat that much squash that often. You'll get the hang of it once you notice which food baby likes best. Then you'll make more of that food and store it in refrigerator jars, conveniently on hand at all times for future meals and in between meal snacks. On the other hand, don't freeze up *too* much food because it's always better to serve food fresh if you have the time each day to make it. Realistically that just isn't possible, as every busy mother knows, so learn how to store fresh foods. (See Food Storage, p. 76, for helpful hints on canning and freezing baby foods.)

MENUS, TO COME

You'll realize in going over the menus in this book that baby's meals are simple. No way do they entail making elaborate seven course banquets. Commercially prepared baby foods sell you on the idea of baby as a gourmet by their fancy-named labels. But nutritious baby meals are not complicated combinations of ingredients and fillers, they are made up of down-to-basic, natural foods. Each takes so little time to prepare for so much nutritional benefit, there's no excuse for not working baby food preparations into your day.

Sample Baby Menus

Now that you know that baby is what baby eats, chances are you're eager and ready to move on to making your own baby food. Yet one last bit of guidance before you squeeze that first orange, peel an overripe banana, or whip up some homemade yogurt: The following sample menus can be used as references for planning balanced meals for baby.

● 2 **months:**

> breast or formula feeding, on demand
> fortified drinks or fruit juice once or twice a day
> yogurt once a day
> fruits twice a day

● 4 **months:**

> as above, plus:
> egg yolk once a day
> cereals twice a day

● 4½-5 **months:**

> as above, plus:
> vegetables once or twice a day
> meat or fowl once a day

● 6-7 **months:**

Around the time baby is being weaned (again, it varies according to each child's needs), a more formal menu schedule can be followed.

Breakfast

citrus juice
egg yolk
fortified milk
cereal (optional)

Lunch

meat or fowl
fruit purée
vegetable
milk

Snack

fortified drink
yogurt

Dinner

fish, fowl, or meat
vegetable
milk
fruit or pudding dessert

Bedtime Bottle

fortified drink
or
fruit juice

● 12 months:

Baby's now really into solids; he's moved on to hunks of meat, slices of cheese, and other nutritious finger foods. The time has come when it's hard to measure accurately the quantity of individual foods baby is consuming, but you can and should keep count of the quality of what baby is eating. As always, filler foods are out, nutritional foods are needed:

Breakfast

fruit juice
egg
cereal
milk
yogurt

Lunch

cheese
green vegetable
meat
milk
fruit dessert

Dinner

meat, fowl, or fish

yellow vegetable
potato
milk
custard, pudding, or fruit ice dessert

Bedtime Snack

finger fruits
milk, fruit juice, or fortified drink
yogurt

● 18 months:

Ideally, once a child is a year and a half he starts on a nutritional menu schedule which he should follow for the rest of his life. Here again, a mother must check her child's daily intake of foods just to be sure he's obtaining all the necessary nutrients:

Breakfast

fruit juice or fresh fruit in season
egg
cereal with milk or yogurt with wheat germ
milk

Lunch

raw vegetables

meat
cheese and fruit dessert

Snack

raw vegetables or fruits
nuts

Dinner

homemade broth
meat, fowl, or fish
vegetables—two varieties
milk or vegetable drink
fruit, custard, or fruit ice dessert

Bedtime Snack

yogurt with fresh fruit purée

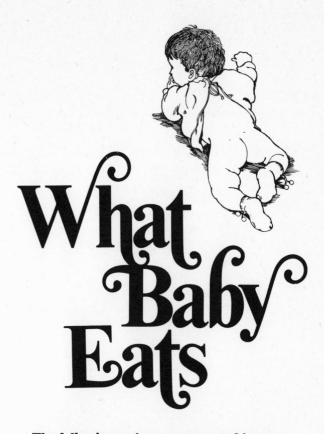

What Baby Eats

The following recipes are presented in age progression from baby's very first fortified drinks to fruits on to meats and fish, his more sophisticated solids. Within each food section, the recipes have been indexed for easy references, according to baby's age and palate sophistication. Each group goes from infant drinks or infant solids (around three to six weeks) to junior foods (around seven months on up to eighteen months, or so).

Baby Drinks: Fruit Juices, Fruit Blends, Milk Pluses, and Milk Shakes

Drinks are introduced to infants at a very young age. At six to eight weeks a child is given his first drink in addition to his breast or his bottle feedings. Don't expect your baby fresh home from the hospital to finish a four-, six-, or eight-ounce bottle of any liquid formula or drink. But a dropper full of diluted fresh orange juice can be worked into baby's daily diet.

Breast fed or bottle fed, a baby soon needs vitamin C. Fresh orange juice is one of the best sources of vitamin C and is therefore the first juice prescribed by pediatricians. For the formula fed child, fresh milk fortified with vitamin D is often the next drink recommended. The drinks in this chapter make excellent transitional foods as the baby goes from a totally liquid diet to solids.

The drink recipes which follow are as simple as slicing and squeezing an orange. Either hand squeeze any fresh citrus fruit (which is a bit laborious) or use an electric juicer or fruit extractor. Once the fresh fruit juice is made, strain it and dilute it with boiled water, bottle, and serve.

Blended drinks take a sophisticated digestive system. Around three months, when baby graduates from round-the-clock breast or formula feedings to some basic solids, he's ready for a fortified drink. Baby will enjoy a milk shake with a solid blended in or a double-up fresh fruit drink. Some drinks need only a dash of honey or a pinch of lime to turn from plain juice or milk to an exciting drink or shake.

These recipes are suggestions rather than formal cooking instructions. Squeeze or blend fruit juices, mix or whip milk drinks and come up with a concoction both delicious and nutritious. Use your imagination.

Remember, fresh fruit is always preferable to canned juice. When fresh fruit is not in season, use fortified frozen fruit concentrates. Vitamin C is destroyed by heat. Therefore any canned juice not refortified with vitamin C (and so stated on the label) has lost all the original nutritional value of the fresh fruit.

A word of warning: Commercial fruit drinks have little nutritional value. Although some are fortified with vitamin C, such drinks are often over-loaded with sweeteners and food colorings. Don't use commercial fruit drinks as fresh fruit juice or frozen fruit juice concentrate substitutes.

These drinks are a new food experience for baby. To help him enjoy it, give him a nice secure arm to lean on and a warm chest to snuggle up to.

FRUIT JUICES

 ● 3 **weeks:**

Orange Juice

Slice, squeeze, strain oranges. Dilute with boiled water. Use roughly 2 parts juice to 1 part water.

● 8 **weeks:**

Grapefruit Juice

Slice, squeeze, strain grapefruit. Dilute with boiled water. Use 2 parts juice to 1 part water. Add honey to taste (optional).

Apple Juice

Wash and cut 6 apples (leave skin on). Stew in 3 pints of boiling water. Strain off liquid.

FRUIT BLENDS

● 5 months:

Orange Juice Special

1 cup fresh orange juice
½ cup undiluted frozen pineapple concentrate
cracked ice cubes

Blend at highest speed.

Orange/Pineapple/Grapefruit Combo

1 part orange juice
1 part pineapple juice
1 part grapefruit juice

Blend.

Orange Apple Blend

1 cup orange juice
¼ cup grated apple

Blend.

Apple Lemonade

1 cup apple juice
2 tablespoons lemon juice
1½ tablespoons honey

½   cup grated apple (optional)

Blend.

MILK PLUSES

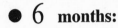 **6 months:**

Milk and Honey

1 cup milk
2 tablespoons honey

Mix.

Molasses Milk

1 cup milk
2 tablespoons molasses

Warm milk. Mix in molasses.

Prune Milk

1 cup milk
2 ounces prune juice

Mix. Serve to constipated child.

No Chocolate Chocolate Milk

1 cup milk
2 tablespoons carob (a natural

sweetener, chocolate-like, rich in calcium, potassium, and phosphorus)

Mix. Serve to (chocolate) allergic child.

NIGHT CAP

● **7 months:**

This stiff drink, a lot of cuddling, some kisses, and a reassuring "I love you" will help your baby sleep through the night, guaranteed. And if you're one of those tired moms who doses off right after the eleven o'clock news, you'll certainly welcome the reprieve from that disruptive mid-night snack.

1	cup milk
½	banana, sliced
¼	teaspoon vanilla
4	tablespoons of homemade yogurt or plain, unsweetened commercial yogurt

Combine all ingredients in a blender. Blend for a minute or two until the banana is smooth and the yogurt curds are well beaten.

Yogurt, Yoghurt, Yoghourt

No matter which way you want to spell it, yogurt is a perfect first food for baby. In fact, it is so easy to digest that yogurt formulas are often given to premature babies whose digestive tracts are particularly sensitive. Because of the valuable bacteria content it is well tolerated by infants who are ill, have diarrhea, constipation, allergies, or colic. But yogurt isn't for the weak or immature digestive systems alone. Healthy babies, Superbabies without digestive problems, love yogurt.

There's more to yogurt: It's made up of living organisms, lactobacillus bulgaricus, which help the body produce B vitamins. It contains bacteria which break down milk sugar into lactic acid, in which disease-producing and gas-forming bacteria can not live. And yogurt is protein.

The Bulgarian peasants are credited with discovering yogurt centuries ago. With a lot of yogurt, very few vegetables, and not much meat at all in their daily diets, Bulgarians have broken all geriatric records, many living on to well over one hundred years old. So feed baby yogurt and send him on his way to a centennial birthday.

Besides containing valuable bacteria, producing B vitamins and vitamin K and eternal life, yogurt also has other things going for it:

—Yogurt is a good food for traveling; kept in a precooled thermos, you can remove as much as is needed and serve to baby.

—Yogurt is an excellent base food for other baby foods as it can be mixed with fruits, vegetables, meats, fish.

—Yogurt's custard-like consistency can be liquified easily by putting it through a blender or stirring it well with a spoon.

—Yogurt can be spoon fed to baby, bottle fed to infants, served as a breakfast, lunch, or dinner food or as a between-meal snack.

—Yogurt can be used for cooking. Freely mix room temperature yogurt with hot food. Just be sure not to boil it away.

SOME WAYS WITH YOGURT

 **weeks:**

Yogurt Alone

2 tablespoons for infants
¼-½ cup for babies 6 weeks on up
1 cup daily for adults

 **months:**

Yogurt to Drink

1 cup milk
½ cup yogurt

Blend.

Yogurt with Frozen Fruit Juice

2 tablespoons undiluted frozen
fruit juice concentrate
½ cup yogurt

Blend.

● 7 **months:**

Yogurt with Fresh Fruit Purée

Two parts yogurt to 1 part any fresh fruit purée.
Mix.

Yogurt Surprise

½ cup yogurt
2   tablespoons honey

Swirl honey once through yogurt to make a marbleized effect.

● 12 months:

Yogurt Pudding

Freeze yogurt until mushy. Remove from freezer and beat with any fruit purée (1 part purée to 2 parts yogurt). Serve.

● 18 months:

Yogurt on a Stick

Stir yogurt until almost liquid. Put in popsicle molds in freezer. Serve with 1 large bib and plenty of napkins on hand. It's messy, all right.

Yogurt is also delicious mixed in desired quantities to taste with:

>   vegetable purée
>   meat purée
>   fish mousse

or top on:

bake-a-potato
baby cereals
baby soups, broths, or skimmed
    natural gravy
baby casseroles
eggs, semi-hard-boiled to scrambled.

Hello Fruits

At six to eight weeks baby's eating a banana. A month thereafter he can move on to other baby fruits. Fruits are baby's first solids. They're mother's way of welcoming baby into the grown-up eating world.

After the banana baby'll love his applesauce. Some like it cooked, some like it raw. Then he's ready to take on fresh fruit purée. Around his first birthday your baby will prefer his fruit in junior finger fruit form.

Buy fruits in season. Be sure they are thoroughly ripened: bananas with brown spots on the skin; melons, peaches, pears, prunes, and plums soft to the touch; pineapples and oranges smelling of fruity fragrances; apples ripe and firm, not mealy; and apricots nice and plump. Fruits organically grown, pesticide free and left to ripen on tree or vine are nutritionally best. But you may need to grow your own to get them in this perfect shape.

Fresh raw fruits blended, cut, or squeezed are ideal baby foods as any cooking, even stewing slightly, destroys some nutrients. When babies find raw fruits too laxative, and they often do, mommies must stew the fruits. Cooking fruits to preserve nutrients is a bit tricky. Use only the smallest amount of water in a saucepan, just enough to stew the fruits without scorching. Cook but a short time, or again you'll render them nutritionless. Keep what cooking liquids remain. They contain valuable nutrients, make excellent baby drinks, can be used for puréeing stewed fruits and other foods.

Fruits are baby's source of carbohydrates, his energy booster. They contain vitamins C and A, too. So use fruits as sweeteners instead of nutritionless refined sugars. Even bake using sweet fruits and vegetables for sweeteners.

Children never outgrow fruits. Infants do lose interest in certain baby foods but fruits continue to please them. Before you know it, you'll be packing fruits in his lunch pail.

BABY'S FIRST FRUITS

apple
apricot

banana
melon
orange
peach
pears
pineapple
prune

THE BASIC BANANA: BABY'S VERY FIRST FRUIT

Buy bananas yellow, never green. Store out of the refrigerator in closed brown bag until the skin is dotted with brown spots. When fully ripe, the fruit reaches its peak of nutrition, high in vitamins A, B, and C, and is easiest for baby to digest. A banana is a simple baby food to prepare—just peel, mash, and serve. Mashed, it's the right consistency to blend in with other baby foods.

● 6 weeks to 2 months:

Banana

½ banana

Cut, peel, and mash with fork or spoon.

● 4 months:

Banana Plus

½ banana
1 teaspoon brewer's yeast

Cut, peel, and mash banana. Stir in yeast.

Banana and Wheat Germ

½ banana
1 tablespoon wheat germ

Cut, peel, and mash banana. Sprinkle with wheat germ.

Banana and Juice

½ banana
2 tablespoons fresh juice

Cut, peel, and mash banana. Mix in juice.

● 6 months:

Banana and Milk

½ banana
1 cup milk

Cut and peel banana. Blend with milk. Mix with cereal or give as a drink.

Banana and Egg Yolk

½ banana
1 semi-hard-boiled egg yolk
   (see p. 116)

Cut and peel banana. Mash together with yolk.

Banana and Yogurt

½ banana
¼ cup yogurt

Cut, peel, and mash banana. Mix in yogurt.

Banana, Egg Yolk, and Yogurt

½ banana
1 semi-hard-boiled egg yolk
   (see p. 116)
¼ cup yogurt

Cut and peel banana. Mash together with yolk. Mix in yogurt.

Banana Applesauce

½ banana
¼ cup homemade applesauce
   (see p. 108)

Cut, peel, and mash banana. Mix in applesauce.

● 12 months:

Banana Fingers

1 banana

Peel banana. Slice lengthwise and serve as finger food.

APPLESAUCE

Applesauce, like all other fruit, is easiest for infants to digest when cooked. By the time baby is about four months old, he'll be able to eat applesauce raw. Either way, it's quick to prepare. When making applesauce, always include the skins in order to retain the nutritional value of the fruit. The skins are the apple's storage source of potassium and vitamin A. Make up large batches of applesauce at one time to have on hand for mixing with fruit purées and juices. It may take you some extra time today but will save you plenty for a busy tomorrow.

● 3 months:

Applesauce, Cooked

Use 2, 4, 6 (however many) cooking apples— Baldwin, McIntosh, Northern Spy, Winesap are the best for this recipe. Slice apples. Core. Place in saucepan, adding water to cover bottom of pan. Cover and steam over low heat for 10 minutes, or until apples are soft. Remove apples with slotted spoon. Put through food mill; skins will remain in mill. If blended, cooked applesauce must be strained to remove the hard to digest skins.

● 4 months:

Applesauce, Raw

Use 2, 4, 6 eating apples such as Golden Delicious or Red Delicious. Measure ¼ cup or so of apple juice. Slice apples. Core. Blend with juice, enough to make sauce moist and smooth.

Fresh Fruit Purée

By blender: Prepare (cut, slice, peel, core, pit) fruit. Steam until tender. Put in blender. Purée.

By food mill: Slice fruit. Steam until tender. Grind in a food mill; seeds, pits, core, and skins will remain in the mill.

● 6 months:

Prune Whip

6 prunes
2 tablespoons milk or formula

Steam prunes. Remove pits. Purée through food mill or in blender. Fold milk or formula into prune purée. Chill.

Peach or Pear Puff

6   peaches or 2 pears
½   cup milk

Wash peaches. Place in small bowl and blanch to remove skins. Pit. Slice into blender. Purée. Or, if you use pears: Steam pears in saucepan. Peel, core, slice. Purée in blender. Add milk to fruit in blender. Whip. Scoop the light, airy, fluffy, puffy mixture into baby's dish. Chill before serving.

Orange Apricots

½   cup apricots
2   tablespoons orange juice

Pit apricots. Steam in saucepan with small amount of water until tender. Remove apricots with slotted spoon. Blend with orange juice. Serve.

● 12 months:

Finger Fruits

When baby gets old enough to start feeding himself, bring out the fruits. Don't cut the fruits, as you would for the rest of the family, into melon balls, pineapple cubes, and banana rounds. Slice fruits into "fingers," length-wise, to make it easier for baby to handle. And use only the very ripe fruits (they mash best between toothless gums), topped with a dash of lemon or pineapple juice to keep fruit from darkening.

Baby's fresh finger fruits can be marinated just like the big guys. Mom and dad may prefer a little liqueur or wine mixed in, but for baby some undiluted frozen fruit juice adds about the same zest.

Use apples, bananas, melon (in season), peaches, pears, and plums. Prepare fresh fruit (peel, core, skin). Cut into "fingers." Mix in finger bowl. Add about 2 tablespoons of undiluted frozen orange juice and mix with fruit until well melted. Sprinkle with citrus or pineapple juice. Chill until fruit has absorbed the marinade. Ready to serve.

● 16 months:

Vermont Maple Baked Apple

Once baby's using a spoon as it should be used, to eat with not to bang with, let him try this easy-to-make baked apple.

> **1** baking apple (Rome Beauty or Jonathan)
> **1** tablespoon maple syrup

Preheat oven to 350°. Core apple. Cut a cavity out of one end of the apple. Cover bottom of baking pan with water ¼ inch deep. Put apple in pan, cavity side up. Fill cavity with maple syrup. Bake uncovered 45 minutes to 1 hour, until apple is pierceable. Occasionally baste apple with maple syrup juice from bottom of pan while cooking. When done, maple syrup in cavity will get candy-like. Let cool slightly before serving.

● 18 months:

Fruit Tops

Many fruits stewed in a bit of water and honey will leave a syrupy liquid, perfect for making fruit toppings. The cooked fruit is then puréed to a pulp, returned to the cooking liquids, and stirred over a low flame until well mixed. What you get is a fruit topping similar to the commercial ones but without extra heavy sweeteners and artificial flavorings. These can be used on top of cereals, mixed into yogurt, or sprinkled over ice creams. Those fruits which seem to lend themselves naturally to toppings are apples, apricots, peaches, and plums.

Cut fruit, remove seeds, and place in saucepan with enough water to cover bottom of pan. Stir in 4 tablespoons of honey. Cover and simmer over a low flame for 10 minutes, checking often to see that honey does not burn. Remove fruit, purée in blender or food mill. Return purée to saucepan, heat, and mix with syrup.

Eggs and Eggs In Things

Did you know that

4–6 whole eggs
or
8–10 egg whites
or
12–14 egg yolks
equal
1 cupful of eggs?

Well, they do. Other facts of eggs are: A tablespoon or so of vinegar dropped into a pan of water before boiling an egg keeps the shell from breaking; eggs covered in the refrigerator won't pick up the smells of other foods; and cook only in stainless steel, for eggs boiled in aluminum pans will turn the pan black.

At about four months old a child will need iron.

He can get it from eggs. All in all eggs have a pretty impressive nutritional track record. They're rich in protein, potassium, sodium chlorine, phosphorus, and vitamins A, B, and D. Eggs are high in iron, so much needed by the very young. You might want to throw some finely ground egg shells into your toddler's meal. Shells are a cheap and valuable source of calicium.

Eggs are easily put into other things. Eggs in milk make a fortified eggnog for a finicky youngster who suddenly refuses to eat solids. Eggs boiled, poached, scrambled, and sunny side up are meals infants, juniors, and family share alike. They're also the basis of many gourmet dishes like egg toast, crêpes, and crème caramel. When baby eats the same meal as family, it makes feeding time easy on busy mommy.

Eggs are one of the bargain foods. At the highest market price per dozen, they're very cheap per pound compared to other high protein foods.

With all these good qualities there are a couple of sour notes. Raw eggs or undercooked egg whites can produce allergic reactions such as nausea, vomiting, diarrhea, and skin rashes. Therefore pediatricians often recommend introducing eggs into baby's diet with cooked yolks only.

Cooking eggs is no big deal. What could be easier than boiling, poaching, scrambling, or throwing an egg in a cup of milk to make a custard? Not much really, but there are special little tricks we'll give you here.

● 4 months:

Eggnog, Cooked

For the very young:

>   **1** cup milk or formula
>   **1** egg beaten

In a saucepan, bring milk up to boiling point. Add beaten egg, stirring constantly. Once thoroughly mixed in, pour eggnog into bottle. Cool before serving.

● 12 months:

Eggnog, Raw

For the year-olds on up:

>   **1** cup milk
>   **1** egg yolk
>   **1** teaspoon honey or pure vanilla
>
>   Blend. Best tasting refrigerator cold.

● 5 months:

Semi-Hard-Boiled Egg Yolk

For baby, an egg yolk should be well cooked, yet moist, not dry. To get the perfect yolk, try this 4 minute egg:

Place egg in small saucepan; cover it with cold water. Bring water to a boil. Once boiling, time egg at a simmer for 4 minutes. Remove egg, run under cold water. Peel away shell. The white will be hard, easy to separate from just-right yolk. Discard white. Mash yoke.

● 6 months:

Poached Egg

Bring water to boil in a small saucepan. Break egg into boiling water. Let set, about 2 or 3 minutes. Remove with slotted spoon. Mash.

● 12 months:

Eggs Brouillés

Scrambled eggs the French way means preparing eggs without any additional ingredients added *before* cooking. By adding liquids *after,* the cooked eggs will not turn watery. If done right, these scrambled eggs will be creamy with soft curds, almost cottage cheese-like in texture.

>   **1** egg
>   **1** teaspoon butter
>   **1** tablespoon whole milk

Beat egg in a small bowl. Melt the butter in an enameled saucepan over low heat. Pour in egg. Stir constantly. It will take some time but as soon as the egg begins to cook, remove it from the heat. The egg will finish cooking off the flame, thickening in the hot pan. Stir in milk to stop the cooking process and to get the right consistency.

● 16 months:

Egg Bull's Eye

>   **1** tablespoon butter
>   **1** slice bread
>   **1** egg

In a one-egg frying pan, melt butter until it bubbles. Cut out a circle in the center of the bread, using an upside-down water glass or cookie cutter. Place bread in pan; crack egg into center hole of bread. Fry on both sides until bread is toasted and egg is firm. When done, the egg toast will have the texture of French toast and look not unlike it. Serve. With a fork or spoon, even a finger will do, let junior have the fun of hitting the bull's eye!

BABY'S BRUNCH

Some days (few though they may be) your baby will sleep late, believe us. And when he does he'll probaby set off his eating schedule. He'll wake famished because he's missed his breakfast. But if you feed him right then, say, ten, ten-thirty, or even as late as eleven, he won't be ready for lunch at noon.

What to do? Why not feed him brunch? It will satisfy his ravenous hunger, plus, if you give him a nutritionally well-balanced meal, it will provide him with those nutrients he might miss when he skips lunch.

Baby's brunch needn't differ much from that of the rest of the family. Serve him a poached egg on cereal (oatmeal, for example), topped with fruit purée. Eating brunch, baby will get his necessary proteins, vitamins, and minerals.

● 18 months:

Soggy French Toast

It's curious that French toast is considered by Americans to be a bona fide French dish. (It isn't, no more than pizza is Italian or Americanized chow mein is authentic Cantonese.) As unFrench as French toast might be, it is still made and served in homes across the U.S.A. The following recipe has been adapted in ingredients and texture to please even the littlest member of the family. That means, of course, making this French toast on the soggy side.

> 1 egg
> ¾ cup milk
> 2 slices bread
>   sugar, cinnamon (optional)

Beat egg and milk together with a fork. Trim the crust from the slices of bread. (Try French bread to make this toast. You'll find it comes out fluffy, puffy, and much more enticing to eat if your baby's at fondle-the-food-with-finger stage.) Soak the bread in the egg-milk mixture, perforating it with a fork so that most of the liquid is absorbed. In a small frying pan, cook the bread in a tablespoon of butter. Be sure *not* to let the toast get brown or very dry.

Serve it a bit undercooked, on the mushy side, which baby will find easier to eat and swallow.

Somewhere Between a Crêpe and a Pancake . . .

there's a galette. Loosely translated, a galette is a broad flat pie. "Flat" is the key to this "pie" which has all the qualities of a crêpe—light, thin, delicate, plus it can be served like a pancake. A galette is so flat, in fact, that the French borrow the word for an expression they have to flatter slim friends: "Tue es plate comme une galette!" Or, as we would put it: "You're as flat as a board!"

A nine- or ten-month old baby will enjoy this pancake. Its crispness makes the galette a good food for teething while at the same time its wafer-like texture makes the galette easy to chew and swallow. Of course if your baby's teeth erupt early, say, six months or so, there's no reason why you can't feed him a galette then. And while you're at it, why not pass some around to the rest of the family?

½ cup flour
½ cup whole milk
2 eggs
pinch nutmeg
½ stick butter

Preheat oven to 425°. Make a lumpy batter by mixing slightly the first three ingredients. Stir in the nutmeg if you plan to serve the galette to the rest of the family. In a 12-inch skillet, melt the butter. When pan is hot, pour in batter. Bake in the oven for 20 minutes. Galette will be ready to serve when golden brown.

For baby: Slice a piece, like a pie, and let it cool before serving. Baby will enjoy the galette best if he's left to eat it from his hands.

For family: Top each piece with a sprinkle of sugar and lemon. Then serve it hot with maple syrup or marmalade.

Quickie Custard

A custard is a great place to sneak in an egg and get some extra milk down junior.

½ cup milk
1 egg yolk
⅛ cup raw sugar (optional)
¼ teaspoon vanilla (optional)

Preheat oven to 350°. Scald milk in small saucepan. In mixing bowl, beat egg yolk with fork. Stir in sugar and vanilla. Pour egg-sugar-vanilla mixture into milk. Stir over heat until liquid slightly thickens. Pour cooked mixture into custard cup. Place in pan of 1 inch of hot water. Bake 45 minutes. Refrigerate. Unmold to serve.

Cereals, Porridges, and Plain Ol' Gruel

Ceres, the goddess of grain and agriculture in Roman mythology, gave her name to cereal. And chances are when she did, cereal was a fine, nutritious food served very much in its natural state as rice, rye, maize, or oats. But that was a couple of centuries B.C. or so before commercial cereals were introduced.

Today, among the instant, polished, refined, commercial cereals are the precooked baby cereals. They are actually worse off nutritionally than those adult dry cereals that go "snap, crackle, and pop!" In both, nutrients have been destroyed by excessive heat processing. In precooked baby cereals, there's also a high content of salt added. And, as the essential nutrients have been milled away, the cereals become merely tummy fillers, not nourishment for growing babies. Sadly, such empty calorie cereals are often introduced to infants as early as six weeks old.

Cereals needn't be given to baby until his fourth month. Even then, limit the cereal repertoire to those from the nutritional stock: oats, wheat, millet, kasha, cornmeal, rice, or enriched farina. (All can be enhanced by natural fortifiers like yogurt, molasses, brewer's yeast, or wheat germ.) And for baby's sake, avoid any cereals that contain bran, as it is irritating to young digestive tracts.

Cook the recommended cereals an extra 5 minutes or so in the top of a double boiler. Cover and let stand over a low heat for a few minutes more than directions suggest. The cereals will retain their original nutritional value but will have the consistency of pudding. That, plus some extra milk or fruit juice will make the cereal soft, liquid-y and most digestible for the very young baby.

BEGINNING CEREALS

● **4** months:

Rice Cream

Put brown rice (about ½ cup at a time) into blender. Turn blender to high speed and pulverize rice to a powder. Pour very slowly into the top of a double boiler, 1 part rice powder to 4 parts water (about ¼ cup of rice powder to a cup of water). Cook until creamy, about 10 minutes, stirring constantly to prevent lumps. This recipe makes about a cup of rice cream. As some will be left over, save in a covered container in the refrigerator and warm up for next time.

Banana Oats

½ cup rolled oats
1 cup water, milk, or formula
½ ripe banana
½ cup milk

Grind oats in blender. Mix ground oats and 1 cup of water, milk, or formula in saucepan. Bring to a boil. Simmer for 4 minutes, stirring constantly. Remove from heat. Cover and let stand for 5 minutes longer. Slice banana into blender, add remaining milk. Blend until frothy. When cooked cereal is ready, stir in the banana-milk mixture. Mix until banana oats are soft and mushy.

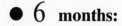 **6 months:**

Swiss Cereal

Birchermuesli, or Swiss Muesli, is a finely ground cereal for infants, originally made in 1895 by a Swiss dietitian, Dr. Bircher-Benner. He advocated feeding children diets rich in fresh fruit; so he devised this cereal made with natural ingredients: appleflakes (the entire apple is used with peel and core so as to retain the apple's original nutritional value), wheat, oat, millet, rye, unrefined sugar, honey, crushed almonds, and wheat germ. It is advisable to add your own fresh fruit as topping. To prepare, mix 4 heaping tablespoons of Swiss cereal with ½ cup of whole milk. Once cereal is completely moistened, add a spoonful of fresh fruit purée or homemade applesauce on top.

Millet Mush

½ cup millet
2 cups water

Stir millet into boiling water in top of a double boiler. Boil for 7 minutes more. Reduce heat and simmer for 30 minutes, or until millet is mush.

HEARTY CEREALS

 8 months:

Cornmeal Meal

½ cup water
¼ cup cornmeal

Bring water to a boil in a small saucepan. Slowly stir in cornmeal. Cook until meal is a mealy mush, about 15 minutes, or so.

● 10 months:

Kasha Gruel

Kasha is made from buckwheat groats, nutritionally high in the B vitamins thiamine and niacin. As a gruel, kasha for breakfast can be made with milk or yogurt, for lunch either straight or with eggs, for dinner mixed in a broth or with meat. It makes a delicious gruel for baby, side dish or casserole for the rest. The amount of times and the variety of ways kasha appears on any family menu is limited only by the cook's imagination.

> ½ (plus) cup kasha
> 1 cup milk
> 1 tablespoon molasses

Grind as much kasha as you wish to make in a blender. Bring milk up to a boil in saucepan. Add enough kasha until liquid thickens to cereal consistency. Cover and cook over low heat for 7 minutes. Stir in molasses. Cool before serving. Store leftovers in jars and refrigerate.

● 12 months:

O-Kayu

O-Kayu is the Japanese's answer to the Jewish Americans' chicken soup. It's not exactly a soup, and it isn't even made with chicken, for that matter. But this rice porridge serves the same purpose: It cheers any baby when he's got the blahs.

½ cup long grain rice or Japanese
     gohan
2 cups water
1 egg
     dash of soy sauce

Mix rice and 1 cup of water in heavy saucepan. Bring to a boil. Stir. Cover. Reduce heat and simmer for 15 minutes. Be sure liquid is totally absorbed. Add an additional cup of water. Recover and simmer for 30 minutes until rice becomes very soggy. While rice cooks, beat egg in a bowl. Mix egg into rice and steam until egg is cooked. Add a dash of soy sauce. The final O-Kayu dish has a gooey, pasty consistency, easy for your under-the-weather child to eat and swallow.

CEREAL TREATS

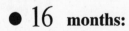 **16 months:**

Oat Cakes

¼ cup butter
     honey to taste

> **1** cup oatmeal

Melt butter. Add honey. Stir in oatmeal. Fry over low heat until oatmeal is brown. Pack into custard cups. Chill. Unmold and serve.

● **18** months:

Farina Forever

Something special is molasses milk and enriched farina, a super-farina everyone will enjoy, forever.

> **1** tablespoon molasses
> **¾** cup milk
> **2** tablespoons enriched farina

Mix milk and molasses in saucepan. Scald milk. Add farina, stirring constantly. Bring to a boil, reduce heat, simmer for a minute or so. Cool before serving.

Vegies

First "yellows" are introduced to baby, as they are the most digestible vegetable. Then "greens" are added to his diet, at about four months. After that, two or more servings of vegetables a day (one from the yellow list, one from the green) are given to baby. With both colors, yellow strong in vitamins, green in minerals, he'll be getting the carbohydrates, vitamins, and minerals he needs.

Buy fresh vegetables. When possible cook them and give them to baby the very same day. The fresher the vegetable, the more nutrients are retained in it. This knowledge, in fact, has set many families to hoeing their own gardens.

Scrub vegetables with a vegetable brush to get them clean of dirt and free of any pesticides. Wash briskly under the faucet. Don't let vegetables sit in water any length of time as it destroys much of the food value. Don't peel off the good vitamins and minerals in the skin of the vegetables. Bake potatoes in the skin, for example, as highest food value lies between the soft inside and the inner part of the skin. Unpeeled beets are cooked with two inches of tops and the roots on. Once cooked, skins usually are puréed with vegetables.

Take special care in cooking baby vegetables. Steam them. Don't overcook them. Save mineral- and vitamin-filled cooking liquids for later puréeing.

Cooked vegetables can be frozen in meal-size portions. It saves time to prepare vegetables in large quantities to freeze for busy days ahead.

BABY'S FIRST VEGETABLES . .

asparagus
beets
carrots
celery
peas
potato
spinach
squash
tomato

● 4 **months:**

Baby's First Vegetables Purée

½   cup chicken or beef broth
1   cup prepared raw vegetables

In a saucepan bring broth with vegetables to a boil. Lower heat, cover. Steam until vegetables are tender. Remove cooked vegetables with slotted spoon. Purée vegetables in blender, gradually adding cooking liquid to get consistency desired.

Baby's First Vegetable Purée Combo

Blend 1 part steamed to 1 part steamed; some suggested combinations follow:

beets and beet tops
carrots and celery
peas and carrots
peas and tomatoes
potatoes and carrots
potatoes and peas
squash and tomatoes

Vegetable Purée Plus

Using vegetable purées as a base, mix in other baby foods:

asparagus and yogurt
beets and yogurt
carrots and applesauce
carrots and egg yolk
celery and cottage cheese
peas and applesauce
peas and cottage cheese
peas and egg yolk
potatoes and yogurt
squash and egg yolk
squash and yogurt
sweet potatoes and banana
tomatoes and cottage cheese
tomatoes and yogurt

● 5 **months:**

Bake-A-Potato

Preheat oven to 350°. Scrub 1 white or sweet potato clean. Bake in jacket to preserve nutrients which are concentrated in the layer directly underneath the skin. Cook for 45 minutes, or until soft when pierced with a fork. Scoop out inside, mash with enough milk to make soft consistency. Serve as is or mix with one of the following:

½ cup yogurt
½ cup cottage cheese
½ cup homemade applesauce
½ mashed banana
½ cup any vegetable purée

● 6 **months:**

Potato Pudding

1 mashed sweet potato
½ cup milk
1 egg

Preheat oven to 325°. Whip potato and milk in blender. Add egg. Blend. Put mixture in small custard cup. Set in water. Bake for 35 minutes until set.

SQUASHED SQUASH

About squash: There are winter squashes, summer squashes, yellow, green, and white squashes. Some squashes are round and scalloped; others are long with crooked necks; some have thin skins, are firm and heavy; while still others have hard shells and extra extra firm rinds. Squashes come in an infinite variety, from the acorn and butternut to the yellow crookneck and zucchini. But the best thing about squashes is that babies love them all. Their choice is indiscriminate. To baby, a squash is a squash as long as it is squashed squash.

Yellow Summer Squash

Preheat oven to 375°. In small baking pan, arrange a layer of thinly sliced squash. Pour ½ cup milk over the squash. Bake covered with tin foil for 15 to 20 minutes. Uncover and bake some more. When ready the squash will be tender and the milk will have set. Cool before squashing with a fork.

Green Zucchini

Wash and slice a zucchini. Place in saucepan with just enough water to cover the bottom. Stir in 1 tablespoon of miso, a nutritious soy paste which can be purchased at health food stores. Cover and steam. When zucchini's pierceable, remove from pan, mash with fork, or put through baby food grinder.

Golden Acorn Squash

Preheat oven to 350°. Cut acorn squash in half and remove seeds and strings. Place right side up in baking dish with water. Cover with tin foil. Bake 35 to 40 minutes, or until tender. For baby: Scoop out pulp and blend with broth, yogurt, or milk. For family: Mix 2 teaspoons raw sugar, 4 teaspoons of butter, and 4 teaspoons of sweet sherry. Pour a spoonful into each acorn cavity. Reheat until sugar melts, then serve.

● 7 months:

Carrot Casserole

1 cup carrot purée
½ cup cottage cheese
   raw wheat germ

Preheat oven to 350°. Mix together carrot purée and cottage cheese. Put in buttered casserole dish. Top with wheat germ to cover. Bake until wheat germ crust is brown.

Celery Slurp

2 large ribs celery
1 cup water
2 tablespoons yogurt

Wash celery, remove strings. Cut celery and place in pan of water. Boil until celery becomes tender. Remove celery with slotted spoon. Whip together celery and yogurt in blender. This celery combo is airy, makes a fluffy textured baby food when blended together with carrots or any other baby vegetable.

Pea Pie

1 cup peas
½ cup applesauce
raw wheat germ

Preheat oven to 325°. Cook peas. Blend with applesauce. Pour into small buttered casserole or custard cups. Sprinkle top with raw wheat germ. Bake 10 to 15 minutes, or until wheat germ is toasted.

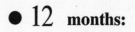 **12 months:**

Borscht

½ cup beet purée
½ yogurt

1 teaspoon lemon juice

Blend all ingredients and chill. Serve as a soup, dinner, or even dessert.

● 16 months:

Stuffed Tomato

Because tomatoes are acidic, they're sometimes tough on sensitive baby skin. The area around the mouth may turn red and slightly sore from tomato dribbles. Therefore, be certain to wash off baby's face with some warm water after a tomato drink or dinner.

1 tomato
¼ cup cottage cheese

Preheat oven to 350°. Wash tomato. Cut top off the tomato and scoop out the pulp. Mix pulp and cottage cheese. Fill cavity with mixture. Bake 15 minutes. For baby: Mash with fork and serve. For family: Sprinkle chives over top of each tomato before serving.

Asparagus

Asparagus is often saved for junior food days. It's

considered too acidic for infants by some nutritionists and has stems which tend to be tough and hard
to digest. When introducing this succulent vegetable
to baby, use only the tips, loved as a delicious
delicacy by both babies and parents alike. Asparagus
tips are the tenderest part of the vegetable and
once steamed slightly can be easily mashed with
a fork. As with tomatoes, be sure to wash junior's
face after asparagus meals. It will save on any
residue aggravation.

Spinach

Spinach is a controversial vegetable, so we're going
to leave the decision of should or shouldn't spinach
be on baby's menu up to you. Spinach's strength-
building reputation aside (it's rich in mineral salts
and vitamins), there remains the fact that spinach is
often loaded with nitrates. Only the spinach grown
organically and sold in health food stores should be
eaten by tiny infants who are most susceptible to
nitrate poisoning. Then it merely takes about 10
minutes of steaming (¼ pound of fresh spinach per
person, per serving) and it's ready to eat. For junior: Blend spinach with its own cooking liquid or
milk. For family: Serve cooked spinach topped with
butter or chips of hard-boiled eggs or raw spinach
as a salad.

AS IS

● 18 months:

Many vegetables can be served as junior foods, as is. They sometimes require no more preparation than a wash, a good scrub with a vegetable brush, and possibly some scraping with a vegetable peeler or slicing with a knife. But don't overlook them just because they're so easy to prepare. They're more often than not the best (nutritionally, palatably, visually, tactually) of baby foods and can double as excellent in-between-meal snacks for the entire family.

At first, use as finger foods those vegetables with which your child is already familiar in purée form, such as carrots, celery, and tomatoes. Then introduce some new ones, for example, cucumbers (peeled, sliced with seeds removed) and mushrooms (washed, sliced with stems removed). Actually, raw vegetables, grated or sliced and fed to a child ten months or older, are preferable to cooked ones. Remember, heat often destroys vegetable nutrients, making cooked proteins, minerals, and vitamins of minimal value.

The Meat Game

Meat will never forget April of '73.

The housewives scored a victory that month when their seven-day boycott against meat resulted in President Nixon's decision to impose a ceiling price on beef, lamb, and pork. Admittedly the housewives hadn't won the game entirely since they had failed to bring the prices down. But as Ralph Nader, the consumer advocate, called the score: "Consumer efforts are not 100 yard dashes; they're marathons."

That same April due to the concerned efforts of nutritionists, scientists, doctors, and well-informed housewives, the meat industry was dealt another blow: The Food and Drug Administration banned the hormone DES used by farmers to speed up the growth of animals and fatten their herds before marketing. DES was known to have caused cancer in test mice and rats. As early as 1960, DES was banned from the production of chickens; now meat was free of it.

Mothers *can* affect change. They *can* insure the right price and the right quality of the meat they feed their children.

Another way that a mother can insure her baby gets the best quality meat is to check the government grade standards on the meat she buys. The three top grades—U.S. Prime, U.S. Choice, and U.S. Good—are the tenderest and leanest meats, well marbleized with nutritious fats. These meats are generally juicy and most digestible if prepared carefully. Tenderness is not a grade factor in the standard measures of poultry. Chickens and turkeys are graded U.S. Grade A, B, or C. Such gradations imply how bruise, tear, and cut free the bird is upon delivery to the market.

Meat and fowl are often introduced into baby's diet well after vegetables, fruits, eggs, and cereals have appeared on the daily menu. Organ meats like liver are most easily digested by a beginning meat eater about three or four months old. (Glandular meats like heart, kidneys, sweetbreads, and brains are perfectly all right for children, it's just that these meats take a lot of time-consuming preparation—trimming cartilage, removing connective tissues. Therefore we have eliminated them from our recipe section with respect to a busy mother's day.) When baby gets a little older, say age six months or so, he will be able to digest ground muscle meat like chopped beef rolled into meatballs. At that time chicken and turkey become part of his menu. At junior age, around ten months, veal and lamb fit into the youngster's diet. No use giving baby pork, ham, or duck. They are greasy, indigestible, packed with cholesterol and unnecessary to his nutrition.

When it comes to meat and babies, here are some basic rules every mother should follow:

1. *To cook meat,* use a dry heat method (roasting, pan-broiling, broiling, and sautéing) for preparing infants' meals. Meats cooked in fats, butters, oils, or rich sauces are too hard for baby to digest. Cook meats at low temperatures to retain natural juices.

2. *To purée meat,* use a blender and mix with meat broths, yogurt, egg yolk, vegetable, or fruit purées to obtain the proper texture. Meat put through a grinder has a tendency to be too grainy, fowl too chalky, to be considered palatable and acceptable by babies.

3. *To store meat,* wrap in loose aluminum foil to allow air circulation and retain freshness. Put meat immediately in the coldest part of the refrigerator. Cook within the next 24 hours. To freeze meat, wrap tightly in aluminum foil to make air tight package. If properly sealed, meat can be frozen and stored at $0°$ up to half a year. Once meat has been cooked and puréed for baby, uneaten portions can be frozen in meal-size servings but must be used within 2 months. Never *re*freeze thawed meats. (That's a rule for anybody's meat, baby's or adult's.)

BABY'S FIRST MEATS

liver
chicken (or turkey)
beef

MEAT BROTHS AND STOCKS

Puréeing Baby's First Meats

Babies like their meats moist. It's virtually impossible to get a baby to eat dry meat without gagging, no matter how finely the meat is puréed. Baby is, after all, admittedly a lazy chewer—partially because he doesn't really know how and more practically because he doesn't have the teeth to chew with. So he wants his meats to be as easy to go down as that yummy slimy banana.

Purée meats for baby with broths or stocks to get the right moist consistency. They can be made in extra large quantities. Once cooked, they should be skimmed before using to prepare baby foods. (To skim: Place liquid in refrigerator until cold; fat will rise to the top and can be easily removed with slotted spoon. Or, refrigerate stock or broth until fat congeals; once solidified, press strips of waxed paper to surface and peel off as fat will adhere to paper.) Store extras in junior-size portions, freeze in ice cube trays. Once frozen, wrap cubes in individual plastic bags. Three or four cubes will yield approximately ⅓ cup of broth. And what a blessing for busy mother to have on hand ready-made cooking liquids and puréeing aides.

Besides their time-saving qualities, chicken, beef, and rich meat broths are all exceptionally nutritious. Cooked with meat bones as the base, vegetables are added to give extra food value. Not only do broths make excellent liquid for cooking and puréeing baby meats but baby vegetables as well. Also use broths and stocks to make baby soups, to make baby gravies, to pour over baby cereals, or to give added zest to any baby meal.

around ● 4 months:

Basic Basic Beef Broth

2½ quarts water
½ tablespoon salt
1 shank bone
1 medium onion, quartered

In a large kettle, pour in water and salt. Wipe bone and pat dry with a paper towel. Put into kettle. Add onion. Bring water to a boil. Cover. Simmer until concentrated (about a quart of liquid), 1½ to 2 hours. Strain broth through sieve or cheesecloth and skim off fat.

Beef Stock

To all ingredients for basic basic beef broth, add cut carrot, diced celery, chopped celery leaves, and chopped parsley. Prepare as for basic basic beef broth. When done, take the bone out of the stock. Scrape off the meat and purée. Scrape marrow from the bones, melt in fry pan with a bit of beef fat. Add meat purée and melted marrow to hot stock. Cool to room temperature. Clarify (strain through cheesecloth) and skim off fat.

Chicken Broth

1	big, old, tough stewing hen
2½	quarts water
1	bunch "soup greens" (leek, knob celery, parsley, carrots)
½	tablespoon salt

Cut up old hen into pieces. Set breast aside. Add all other ingredients to kettle. Bring water to boil. Lower heat, cover, and simmer for 1 to 1½ hours. Cool to room temperature. Clarify and skim. (One half hour before done, add tender breast, which should not be overcooked to the point of becoming tough. Cooked chicken breast can be puréed with broth for a baby meal, or cubed as finger food or sliced to give family in sandwiches or salads.)

Brodo

Brodo, a rich meat broth, is served in every Italian home and every Italian trattoria. Often tortellini (little twisted macaroni stuffed with meat) or pastina (tiny pasta) is added to the broth to make a rich, nutritional soup. This popular dish is easy to make, can be frozen and served at a later date.

1 four-pound chicken split in half or chicken necks, bones, wings, and legs

1 pound lean veal (ask for scraps of veal scallopini which a butcher will give you at a good price)

1 medium onion, cut in half

3 carrots, diced

3 tomatoes, quartered

3 quarts water

Combine all ingredients in a large pot. Bring to a boil. Reduce heat and simmer for 2 hours. Strain and remove fat.

LIVER

Liver is the best known natural source of iron. It is rich in protein, minerals, and all the B complex vitamins. Liver is an organ meat and easier for baby to digest than muscle meats such as beef roasts or chops.

However, liver has come under a great deal of criticism these days, since this glandular organ retains undesirable pesticides, traces of which still remain in the liver. Fortunately, you can buy some liver in health food stores that is pesticide-free. But you're still dealing with a food (organ) that is part of the digestive system. So you have these food facts to weigh when considering feeding your baby liver.

Most mothers and their pediatricians are still swayed in favor of liver because of its nutritional value. We tend to agree. But this is a decision to make with your own doctor. One mother we know, Pauline Crammer, is convinced her daughter, Jennifer, has thrived on it. Jenny started on liver pâté when she was only three months old, loved it, and moved right on to liver mousse and liver loaf. By the time she was ten months old she ate her liver in chunks as she still does today almost six years later, claiming it's "finger lickin' liver good!"

● 4 **months:**

Liver Pâté

½ pound liver

¼ small onion, diced
½ tomato, peeled
½ carrot, diced
¾ cup water or beef broth

Place all solid ingredients in a pan with liquid and bring to a boil. Reduce heat and simmer for 7 to 10 minutes. Scoop out meat and vegetables by adding reserved cooking liquid to blender as needed, a tablespoon at a time. If you wish to fortify with extra B and E vitamins, add ½ teaspoon of wheat germ and ¼ teaspoon of brewer's yeast to the purée. For baby: Serve plain. For family: Garnish with parsley or chopped egg.

Liver Mousse

1 tablespoon cooking oil
½ pound liver
1 egg

Heat oil in pan. Cut away liver membranes. Stir yolk with fork, scramble in with liver. Cook until mixture is firm. Purée in blender. In bowl, whip egg white with whisk. Fold stiff white into liver-egg purée. Pour liver mousse into custard cup. (If you let mousse stand, the egg whites will become runny and separate from the purée; if you refrigerate liver mousse to use later, the liver-egg purée will become unpalatably hard.) Serve liver mousse right away.

● 6 months:

Liver Loaf

1   egg
1   cup raw liver purée
¼ cup milk
¼ cup roasted wheat germ

Preheat oven to 325°. In a bowl, beat egg with fork. Add and mix in all other ingredients. Form into a small loaf and place in a small bread loaf pan. Set pan in another pan with water, and bake like custard in oven until set, about 40 minutes. Serve to baby and family alike.

● 10 months:

Liver Chunks

Liver makes a good junior food. On baby's priority list of likes, it probably runs a close second to banana as a finger food favorite. Liver, like a banana, is smooth and slides down the smallest throats easily with little or no chewing. And, boy, what fun it is to mash, poke fingers into, and throw on the floor! Just one precaution: Cut the liver chunks in smaller than bite-size portions before sautéeing and giving to baby to eat in his hands. You want to be certain that any excited moments of showing off at dinner time won't turn into choking tears.

CHICKEN

Chicken is possibly the mildest meat in taste, the smoothest in texture and the most digestible of all baby foods. It is easy to prepare: Remove membranes, bones, skin, and it's ready to cook. Or use pieces from the already cooked family chicken to make dinner for baby. Puréed with broth, chicken becomes fluffy and smooth, the way babies—especially the younger ones—like their foods best. Double or quadruple the following recipes since cooked chicken stores so well, remains fresh for a long period of time, well up to 2 months. Freeze the uneaten portions in baby-meal-size servings for easy dinners on those overcrowded busy days to come. Then save the serving of chicken pieces, sliced from the breast or left on the thigh, for junior food days.

● 6 months:

Chicken Purée

The Sunday roasted, stewed, or broiled chicken (easy on the salt) can be served up to baby, puréed. Slice off a piece of chicken and remove any skin, gristle, or bones. Cut meat into small bits. Put into blender. Take out of the freezer a few cubes of frozen chicken broth (enough when melted to cover chicken) and warm up in a saucepan until they become liquid. (It's probably best not to use liquid in which the family chicken was cooked as it may be too greasy from the fat in the bird's skin.) Add broth to chicken in blender. Purée.

Chicken Purée with Yogurt

½ cup chicken purée
4   tablespoons yogurt

Blend.

Chicken Purée with Noodles

½ cup chicken purée
½ cup brodo with pastina
(see recipe, p. 145)

Blend.

● 7 months:

Chicken Purée, Peas, and Carrots

½ cup chicken purée

¼ cup peas and carrots purée combo

¼ cup heated chicken broth

Blend.

● 8 **months:**

Chicken Purée Casserole

½ cup chicken purée

½ cup applesauce

¼ cup cooked sweet potato, mashed

Preheat oven to 325°. Mix well chicken purée and applesauce together in bowl. Put mixture in a buttered casserole dish. Cover with mashed potatoes. Bake until potato top turns into golden brown crust.

● 12 **months:**

Chicken Thighs

Preheat oven to 350°. Wash chicken thighs and pat dry with paper towel. Remove skin and dip in milk. Roll thighs in raw wheat germ until coated. Bake for 45 minutes to 1 hour. Give chicken thighs to junior to tackle like a regular King Henry VIII.

(And like King Henry VIII's, we can guarantee this meal will end up on the floor!)

TURKEY

● **14** months:

Turkey is pretty much interchangeable with chicken as a baby food. The subtle differences lie in taste —turkey meat is gamier than chicken, possibly richer to some little people in taste. We'd advise waiting until baby's on to junior foods before treating him to his first turkey meal. By then, it'll only be a matter of slicing some meat from the family bird to prepare junior a turkey treat. Besides, Thanksgiving dinner this year will be better appreciated (and digested) next.

BEEF

As beef is a muscle meat, therefore stringy, tough, and not as easy to digest as organ meats or poultry, it should be well stewed to soften its texture for infant feeding. If you already know how to make your own special stew, use that recipe. The stew we have suggested here has been created with babies first in mind. The sauce is mild, unlike a ragout or a goulash, and the vegetables have been taken from Baby's First Vegetables list (see p. 130). Stewed for an hour or more, the meat becomes so tender it falls apart, and the vegetables end up so mushy you could easily mash with a fork and serve. By the time baby has mastered this hearty beef stew, he'll move on to more elaborate beef meals. When he's about ten months old, he'll like testing his new teeth on ground rather than puréed meat.

● 6 months:

Beef Stew

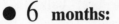

> 2 pounds stew beef, cubed
> 1 quart beef stock
> 2 cups Baby's First Vegetables
> 2 cups tomatoes, slice and peeled

Put all ingredients except tomatoes in cast-iron casserole. Bring to a boil. Cover and put on back burner to stew. Cook over a low flame for 1½ hours. Stir in tomatoes. Cook until tender about 15 minutes more. For baby: Remove solids with slotted spoon and purée with cooking liquid. For family: Serve as is.

● 10 months:

Beef Balls

½ pound ground chuck
1 egg
¼ cup stuffing bread

Mix all ingredients. Form into 1½ inch balls. In heavy skillet, heat 2 tablespoons of vegetable oil. Add meatballs, sauté, and turn with wooden spatula until they become brown on all sides. For baby: Mash with fork and top with fresh tomato purée (optional). For family: Slice beef balls in half, layer on cut loaf of Italian bread. Top with homemade tomato sauce. Serve hot meatball sandwich with brodo (see p. 145) for tummy-warming lunch.

Beef Burger

¼ pound ground steak

Preheat broiler. Form ground meat into a patty. Broil until brown. Turn. Broil until burger is done medium. For baby: Mash. For junior: Give him the patty to eat in his hands.

● 12 months:

Beef Pie

1 pound ground beef

2 tablespoons cooking oil
1 baked potato
½ cup milk
1 egg

Preheat oven to 425°. Sauté ground meat in cooking oil. Scoop out pulp from potato and whip with milk until fluffy. Place the meat in bottom of casserole topped with mashed potatoes. Brush with beaten egg. Bake 15 minutes until potato crust is brown.

JUNIOR MEATS

Once baby has had chopped beef, slices of chicken or turkey, and chunks of liver, he's ready for additional junior meats:

lamb
veal

Lamb can be cut from the family's roast or chops, fat and gristle removed, and chopped into patties for baby. When you buy veal for baby's dinner, ask the butcher to slice some cutlets. They're expensive but lean and tender, easy to chew. All meats, at this stage, can be served to baby as finger foods. Actually, it's advisable since some nutritionists contend that meats cut in small enough pieces to be eaten by baby without choking are a better way of introducing meat proteins. Apparently chunks of meat remain in the stomach longer and are digested more completely than puréed foods.

● 14 months:

Lamburger

1 slice bacon, diced
¼ onion, chopped
¼ pound ground lamb
¼ teaspoon fresh mint, chopped (optional)

Cook bacon in frying pan. Add onion to bacon drippings. Mix and cook until onion is tender. Remove onion and bacon bits with slotted spoon; reserve bacon drippings in fry pan. Mix all ingredients in bowl. Form into patty. Cook lamburger in bacon drippings until well done. Serve without mashing.

● 18 months:

Veal with Lemon

Sauté a pounded-thin veal cutlet in a small amount of cooking oil. Squeeze a little lemon on it. Turn to other side and sauté. Squeeze some more lemon over meat. When veal turns whitish-gray it's done. Cut into junior-size pieces to serve.

Fish Facts and Fantasies

Fish is good for young kids and old fogies because it's low in fat content, easy to chew and digest. The fillet cut is the best part of fish for baby as it is not likely to have bones.

Fish is high in minerals and proteins which help build strong teeth and bones. Fish is also a source of magnesium, phosphorus, iron, copper, and iodine. And some fishes like salmon and mackerel are excellent sources of vitamins A and D.

Buy only fresh fish. Go ahead and smell it to find out if it is *really* fresh. If it's fishy smelling, it isn't. If the fish is odor fresh and mild, if the flesh is firm and elastic, if the eyes are bright and clear, and the gills are reddish and have no slime, then chances are the fish is fresh. And if you are given a fish from a friend who isn't very specific as to when and where the fish was caught (his fish story may seem fishy), check its freshness by placing the fish in cold water. Fresh fish will float.

To cut costs, buy fish "when it runs in season," as a seasoned fisherman would say. Fish in season is available in good supply at the time. Remember, each coastal state has its own fish indigenous to that particular area and season. There's the Baltimore crab, the Long Island blue, the California salmon, and the Rockies rainbow trout. The best bass come from the Great Lakes, lobster from Maine, and pompanos from Florida. Fortunately the "baby fish"—sole, flounder, shad, and whitefish—spawn in many coastal areas. When shopping for fish, keep in mind the initial premise of making your own baby food: Use what's available. That way you'll save yourself time and money.

Contrary to its reputation, fish isn't all that cheap. Even so, it is considered a budget food because, unlike meat, there is never any waste.

Bake, broil, steam, or poach fish for baby. In most fish cooking, it is advisable to turn the fish once when halfway finished cooking. A fish is ready to eat only when cooked all the way through. But at the same time, don't overcook fish because it becomes tough and loses its flavor. Properly cooked fish is firm and flakes easily, ready for baby to eat. Check for doneness as you would with a cake—poke it, and see if the flesh springs back to shape.

Before serving, give a careful last minute check. Rub your fingers through the fish to see that there are no bones. After eating, wash baby's hands and yours in some lemon juice to remove any offensive fishy odors.

BABY'S FIRST FISH

● 7-10-12 months:

sole
flounder
whitefish

Poached Fish

Filleted fish lends itself best to poaching or steaming. It is a tender piece of fish, not thick or steaklike, cut lengthwise away from the side of the fish. To prepare fillet, if you don't have a fish poacher or steamer, use a vegetable steamer. It works just as well. Put steamer in skillet, immerse with fish in liquid, and cover to cook. When done, remove fish from poacher right away or, like a scrambled egg, fish will continue to cook and dry out in the hot pan.

¾ cup chicken broth
4 ounces fish fillet
(sole or flounder)

Boil liquid. Drop in fish (either cut or whole). Immediately turn down heat to simmer. Cook for about 5 minutes, then check for doneness. For baby: Blend with cooking liquids. For junior: Flake with your fingers into small pieces.

Sole Stew

½ cup poached sole
½ cup puréed vegetables
¼ cup milk

Preheat oven to 325°. Blend together all ingredients. Scoop into baking dish. Cook for 15 minutes.

Fish Mousse:
For Baby and Family

1 pound poached whitefish,
trimmed and boned
3 egg whites
1 cup yogurt

Blend all ingredients. Chill well in refrigerator before serving.

Summer Sherbets, Ices, Pops, and, Ice Box Things

There's no doubt about the nutritional value of these ices. Although they are considered "sweets," we include them because they are made with fresh fruit purées and fresh fruit juices. When it comes to make-your-own snow ice, a child can add a nice big glop of molasses or maple syrup for topping.

Count on making these frozen treats over and over again because the demand for them will be great. You might even want to double the recipes so that there'll always be plenty on hand to have for the asking.

SUMMER SHERBETS

● 10 months:

Note: It takes only 45 minutes to 1 hour for freezing sherbets—to set and become firm, when they'll be ready to serve. Any longer than that, sherbets will get too hard to eat.

With Fresh Fruit

1 cup ice cream
1 cup fresh fruit purée

Soften ice cream with a spoon until smooth, almost cream-like. Using a rubber spatula, fold fruit and ice cream together. Freeze.

With Frozen Fruit Juice

1 can undiluted frozen fruit juice
  concentrate
1 cup yogurt

Let frozen juice stand at room temperature until soft but not liquid. Fold juice and yogurt together. Freeze.

● 12 months:

Melon Ice, Pineapple Ice, Apple, Orange, or Peach Ice

Use any one fruit or a combination of several:

½ cup fresh fruit purée
2 cups water

Mix ingredients. Pour into festive colored paper cups (fluted cupcake cups will do), lined up in chilled refrigerator tray. Cover with foil. Place in freezer. To get the right consistency, stir intermittently until crystals form. Freeze 3½ to 5 hours.

● 14 months:

Very Lemony Lemon Ice

In order for this sweet ice to crystallize, never use more or less than 1 part sugar to 4 parts liquid. Or, this Very Lemony Lemon Ice will not solidify and you'll end up with Avgolemono soup.

> ½ cup strained fresh lemon juice
> 1½ cup water
> ½ cup sugar

Mix ingredients until sugar has completely dissolved. Freeze without stirring until crystals form, about 3½ to 5 hours.

● 16 months:

Quick Freeze Cottage Cheese

> 2 tablespoons partially creamed cottage cheese
> 1 apple, peeled, cored, and sliced
> ¼ cup apple juice

Blend ingredients. Pour into chilled custard cups. Freeze 30 minutes (if left to freeze longer, unwanted crystals will form). Serve immediately.

● **18** months:

Fruit Pops

2½ cups any fresh fruit juice
2   cups any fruit purée

Freeze juice to a soft mush. Remove from freezer and fold in fruit. Pour mixture into chilled popsicle molds or ice-cube tray. Freeze partially. Insert popsicle stick in center of each mold or cube. Freeze until solid.

Papa's Fresh Snow Ice Cream

Come winter, try:

About the Snow Ice Cream, I really can't tell you too much because it's no big deal to make. Down home, we first skim off the dirty part of a heavy snow. Then the clean part is used and put in a deep dish. Pour in a small amount of whole milk in proportion. Not too much at first. A little bit of sugar is added to suit the taste, then vanilla flavor. Stir to mix. Guess that's all there is to it!

Love,

Papa

Appendix

Bibliography

Titles marked with an asterisk (*) are available in paperback edition.

Titles marked with a dagger (†) are available as complimentary pamphlets.

American Academy of Pediatrics Committee on Nutrition. "Filled Milks, Imitation Milks, and Coffee Whiteners," *Pediatrics,* 49 (May, 1972): 770–775.

† American Dairy Goat Association. *Dairy Goats Why? What? and How?* rev. ed. Spindale, North Carolina: American Dairy Goat Association, 1969.

† American Dental Association. *Your Dentist Recommends Fluoridation.* Chicago: American Dental Association, 1970.

Brody, Jane E. "Baby Bottle as Pacifier Linked to Tooth Decay," *The New York Times,* December 7, 1972, p. 106.

_____. "Most Pregnant Women Found Taking Excess Drugs," *The New York Times,* March 18, 1973, p. 48.

Brozan, Nadine. "Prepared Baby Food Is Convenient,

But Is It Best for the Child?" *The New York Times,* August 30, 1972, p. 24.

† Burke, Bertha S., and Ruth Roth. *For Parents-to-Be . . . How Food Helps Mother and Baby,* rev. ed. Chicago: National Dairy Council, 1964.

† California State Dairy Goat Council. *Why Goat Milk?* Spindale, North Carolina: American Dairy Goat Assn. (n.d.).

Campbell, Mary Mason. *Betty Crocker's Kitchen Gardens,* New York: Universal Publishing and Distributing Corporation, 1971.

Commoner, Barry. "Nitrate in Baby Food," *Scientist and Citizen,* 10 (January–February, 1968): 13–28.

* Davis, Adelle. *Let's Cook It Right,* rev. ed. New York: Harcourt, Brace & World, Inc., 1962.

* _____. *Let's Have Healthy Children,* rev. ed. New York: Harcourt, Brace & World, Inc., 1959.

Diamond, Howard I., M.D. "Pregnancy and Weight," *Natural Living,* 3 (Fall, 1972): 13–15.

* Eiger, Marvin S., M.D., and Sally Wendkos Olds. *The Complete Book of Breastfeeding.* New York: Workman Publishing Company, Inc., 1972.

Emerling, Carol G., and Eugene O. Jonckers. *The Allergy Cookbook.* New York: Doubleday & Company, Inc., 1969.

Gause, Ralph W. "Problems of Pregnancy," *The PTA Magazine,* 65 (January, 1971): 24–26.

Gilmore, C. P. "The Real Villain in Heart Disease," *The New York Times Magazine,* March 25, 1973, pp. 31 ff.

* Hewitt, Jean. *The New York Times Natural Foods Cookbook*. New York: Quadrangle Books, Inc., 1971.

Hill, Gladwin. "Impure Tap Water a Growing Hazard to the Health of Millions Across U.S.," *The New York Times,* May 13, 1973, pp. 1, 50.

* Hirschfeld, Herman, M.D. *Your Allergic Child*. New York: Arc Books, Inc., 1970.

* Hunter, Beatrice Trum. *Consumer Beware!* New York: Simon and Schuster, Inc., 1971.

* _____. *The Natural Foods Cookbook*. New York: Simon and Schuster, Inc., 1961.

_____. "Put a Bloom on Children," *Natural Living,* 3 (Fall, 1972): 51.

* Jacobson, Michael F. *Eater's Digest: The Consumer's Factbook of Food Additives*. New York: Doubleday & Company, Inc., 1972.

Johnson, Roberta (ed.). *Mother's in the Kitchen*. Franklin Park: La Leche League International, 1971.

Kenda, Margaret, and Phyllis Williams. "Real Home-made Baby Food," *Natural Living,* 1 (Fall, 1972): 42–44, 48.

Knox, Richard A. "Malnutrition Hits U.S. Mothers-to-Be," *The Kansas City Star,* January 15, 1973, p. 6.

_____. "What a Woman Eats Affects Unborn Child," *The Kansas City Star,* January 12, 1973, p. 10.

* La Leche League International. *The Womanly Art*

of Breast Feeding, 2nd ed. Franklin Park: La Leche League International, 1963.

* Larson, Gena. *Better Food for Better Babies.* New Canaan: Pivot Original Health Books, 1972.

Liley, Margaret, M.D., and Beth Day. "The Secret World of the Unborn Baby," *Woman's Day,* May, 1968, pp. 58–60, 106–109.

* Longgood, William. *The Poisons in Your Food.* New York: Simon and Schuster, Inc., 1960.

Lyons, Richard D. "Sugar in Almost Everything You Eat," *The New York Times,* March 11, 1973, p. 10.

* Macia, Rafael. *The Natural Foods and Nutrition Handbook.* New York: Perennial Library, 1972.

† March of Dimes. *Be Good to Your Baby Before It Is Born.* White Plains: The National Foundation– March of Dimes (n.d.).

† ————. *Nutrition & Birth Defects Prevention.* White Plains: The National Foundation–March of Dimes (n.d.).

† ————. *Unprescribed Drugs & Birth Defects Prevention.* White Plains: The National Foundation–March of Dimes (n.d.).

Mayer, Jean. "Watch Your Diet and Live," *The New York Times Magazine,* April 8, 1973, pp. 72 ff.

† McEnery, E. T., M.D., and Margaret Jane Suydam. *Feeding Little Folks.* Chicago: National Dairy Council, 1967.

Milkie, Ron. "Chickens and Eggs," *Natural Life,* 1 (October, 1972): 28–29, 62.

Nader, Ralph. "Baby Foods: Can You (and Your

Baby) Afford Them?" *McCall's*, 98 (November, 1970): 36, 116.

† National Dairy Council. *Feeding Your Baby at Your Breast*, rev. ed. Chicago: National Dairy Council, 1965.

† _____. *Feeding Your Baby During His First Year*. Chicago: National Dairy Council, 1972.

† _____. *Milk . . . . . its food value*, rev. ed. Chicago: National Dairy Council, 1971.

† _____. *Newer Knowledge of Milk*, 3rd ed. Chicago: National Dairy Council, 1972.

† _____. *When Your Baby Is Bottle Fed*. Chicago: National Dairy Council, 1968.

* Pomeranz, Virginia E., M.D., and Dodi Schultz. *The Mother's Medical Encyclopedia*. New York: New American Library, 1972.

Ribble, Margaret A., M.D. *The Rights of Infants*, 2nd ed. New York: Columbia University Press, 1965.

* Richmond, Sonya. *International Vegetarian Cookery*. New York: Arco Publishing Company, 1972.

* Rombauer, Irma S., and Marion Rombauer Becker. *Joy of Cooking*. Indianapolis: Bobbs-Merrill, 1962.

Sasanow, Richard, and April Koral Sasanow. "Chug-A-Lug a Yoghurt," *Natural Living*, 4 (Spring, 1973): 10–12 ff.

* Skreczko, Lynne. *Getting Into Health Foods*. New York: Lancer Books, 1973.

* Smetinoff, Olga. *The Yogurt Cookbook*. New York: Pyramid Publications, 1971.

Soltanoff, Jack, H.M.D., D.C. "Breastfeeding," *Natural Living,* 3 (Fall, 1972): 10–12, 72.

* Spock, Benjamin, M.D. *Baby and Child Care,* rev. ed. New York: Hawthorn Books, Inc., 1968.

* ————. and Miriam E. Lowenberg, Ph.D. *Feeding Your Baby and Child.* New York: Duell, Sloan and Pearce, 1955.

* Turner, James S. *The Chemical Feast: Ralph Nader's Study Group on the Food and Drug Administration.* New York: Grossman Publishers, Inc., 1970.

* United States Department of Agriculture. *Composition of Foods, Agriculture Handbook No. 8.* Washington, D.C.: U.S. Government Printing Office, 1963.

* ————. *Milk in Family Meals: A Guide for Consumers, Home and Garden Bulletin No. 127,* rev. ed. Washington, D.C.: U.S. Government Printing Office, 1972.

* ————. *USDA Grade Standards for Food—How They Are Developed and Used.* Washington, D.C.: U.S. Government Printing Office, 1973.

* United States Department of Commerce. *Common Sense Fish Cookery, Fishery Market Development Series No. 13.* Washington, D.C.: U.S. Government Printing Office (n.d.).

* United States Department of Health, Education and Welfare *Salmonella & Food Poisoning.* Washington, D.C.: U.S. Government Printing Office, 1972.

Wessel, Morris A., M.D. "Weaning Made Easy," *Parents Magazine,* 47 (December, 1972): 40–41 ff.

Wurster, Charles F. "DDT in Mother's Milk," *Saturday Review* (May 2, 1970): 58–59.

General Index

Index of Food and Recipes